WHEELER'S · NEW FISH COOKERY

Wheeler's
NEW FISH COOKERY

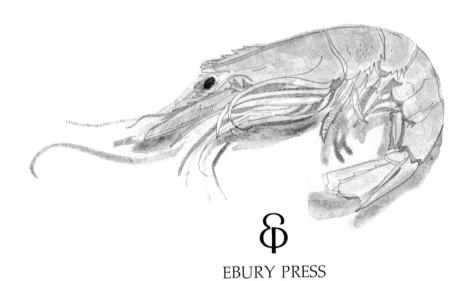

EBURY PRESS
LONDON

Published by Ebury Press
Division of The National Magazine Company Ltd
Colquhoun House
27–37 Broadwick Street
London W1V 1FR

First impression 1986

ISBN 85223 541 0

Editor   Barbara Croxford
Designer   Ted McCausland
Photographer   James Murphy
Illustrators   Linda Smith, Ron Hayward

Filmset by Advanced Filmsetters (Glasgow) Ltd.
Printed and bound in Italy by New Interlitho, S.p.a., Milan.

CONTENTS

A BRIEF HISTORY
of
WHEELER'S

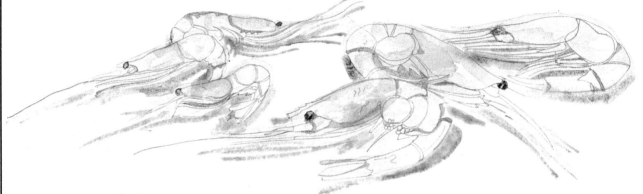

*F*or many people, the name of Wheeler's is synonymous with oysters. This is hardly surprising, since the reputation of this historic fish restaurant was founded on the delectable shellfish.

The name Wheeler's is actually derived from a rather shadowy, Dickensian character called Captain Wheeler who, in 1856, set up an oyster bar in East Anglia. But the Wheeler's of today owes more to Bernard Walsh who bought the old captain's shop and, with it, the name. It was this name that he therefore used when he moved to London to set up a wholesale fish business, just after the First World War—a time of severe depression and unemployment but nevertheless a period when business premises were relatively cheap and easy to come by. He chose a shop in Old Compton Street, from where his first order—some four and a half thousand prime oysters—was despatched by tricycle to the Café de Paris, the Criterion Brasserie and the Blue Train, the most fashionable restaurants of the day.

Public demand for seafood grew, and in 1929 Wheeler's entered the retail trade. The first oyster bar, still on the ground floor of the tiny Old Compton Street premises, soon became *the* place to eat oysters. Prices ranged from 2/6d for the cheapest to 7/6d a dozen for the very best Royal Whitstables and Colchesters. Most customers apparently favoured the green-bearded Essex at 3/6d, followed by a slice of the very best cheeses.

Having their own wholesale supply, the high quality of Wheeler's produce was guaranteed, and soon the bill of fare was extended to include Dover sole, lobster, crab and smoked salmon. During the '30s, however, oysters remained the main attraction for customers and in the oyster season Bernard Walsh and his wife kept Wheeler's open from 8am. to midnight every day of the week. After 1945, when other foods were still in short supply, Wheeler's became even more popular as Londoners and visitors flocked there for a taste of gourmet living after years of drab austerity.

It was in this new mood of luxury, and a certain frivolity, that the Thursday Club was born. In 1946, the new editor of 'The Tatler', Sean Fielding, told his contributors that they could meet him, not at the office, but rather at luncheon each Thursday at Wheeler's, Old Compton Street. These small gatherings soon grew into an elite club, about which many an outrageous tale has been circulated. The true story is probably no more disreputable than the slightly riotous behaviour to be expected when a group of creative 'Bohemians' get together for a spot of over-indulgence. There were no political over-tones, no club rules, just the enviable object of extending the British weekend from Thursday to Tuesday. The club now only meets monthly and rarely extends beyond Thursday. The famous publication 'Wheeler's Review' was first produced by one of the founder members of the Thursday Club, the brilliant cartoonist Anthony Wysard. This sophisticated magazine, containing articles by some of the best writers and artists of the day, has a world following.

Providing fixed-rate lunches for such a dedicated band of eaters and drinkers as the Thursday Club cannot have been a profitable proposition, but there can be little doubt of its long-term value. The members' demands, not only for the very best seafood, but for new ways of preparing and serving it, was the stimulus for a new Wheeler's. Superb dishes demand superb chefs, and Bernard Walsh acquired one—a certain Mr. Song, who had been *saucier* at both the Café de Paris and the Kit Kat Club. At this point Wheeler's began to grow from oyster bar to restaurant.

The only problem for customers was getting a table. So, in 1949, Wheeler's moved from their first, modest premises to the elegance of St. James's. This restaurant soon became even busier than the first, and within three

years another—the Vendôme—was opened, this time in Mayfair. A year later came the Carafe in Belgravia, followed two years after that by the Antoine in Charlotte Street. In the thriving '50s, the most fashionable addition to the family was The Ivy, a favourite meeting place for actors and their audiences. The Ivy left the organisation for a time but rejoined the Wheeler's fold to much acclaim in 1984.

In 1967, Wheeler's had an immediate success with the Alcove in Kensington High Street and this was followed by premises in the City, Brighton, Blackheath, Highgate, Harrow, Woodstock and Beaconsfield, all bearing the unique mark of Wheeler's.

Each Wheeler's establishment is chosen with care, and reflects the tradition of excellence for which they are famous. A charming feature they all share is the abundance of interesting works of art—some quite fine—which give to each a unique character. A regular visitor to more than one Wheeler's will soon note that each restaurant has its specialities. At Old Compton Street, for instance, visitors enjoy an eclectic array of prints, china and oil paintings. The diners may also find themselves sitting on one of the restaurant's original 16 chairs bought in 1929 for 7/6d a piece.

With the trend towards healthier eating, people are beginning to realise the value of fish. Delicious, rich in vitamins and minerals, and low in saturated fats, it is one of the very best 'whole' foods there is. Cooked in the Wheeler's way, it can have few rivals.

WHITE FISH

This fish group includes a wide variety of fish, ranging from everyday cod to the much prized Dover sole. White fish falls into two categories—round fish and flat fish—but if you would like to ring the changes in a recipe, you will find that white fish within the same group are readily interchangeable. For example, cod has several members in its family, including hake, haddock, coley and whiting, and you can substitute any of these in cod recipes.

Two of the finest-flavoured sea fish—sole and turbot—belong to the flat fish group. Dover sole, in particular, has always fired the imagination of chefs, and a sumptuous selection of Wheeler's recipes is included here. Another excellent flat fish is halibut. The largest flat fish available, it is sold in fillets or steaks.

This section includes a wealth of varied recipes from soups, kebabs, flans and curries to stir-fries, casseroles, pies, soufflés and simply cooked fish with sauces.

RECIPES

ROUND WHITE FISH

Bass

Huss

Cod

Sea Bream

Grey Mullet

Conger Eel

Ling

Whiting

10

Red Mullet

Coley

Gurnard

Haddock

Hake

Pollack

John Dory

11

FLAT WHITE FISH

Dab

Halibut

Skate

Lemon Sole

Dover Sole

Plaice

Monkfish

Flounder

12

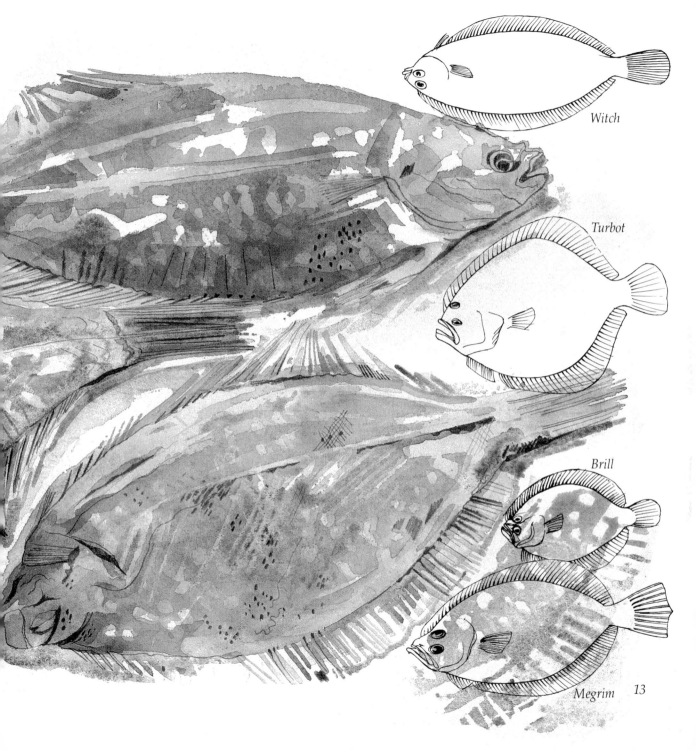

Witch

Turbot

Brill

Megrim 13

Barbecued Bass with Dill Butter

SERVES FOUR

100 g (4 oz) unsalted butter

20 ml (4 level tsp) dried dillweed

finely grated rind and juice of 1 lemon

salt and freshly ground pepper

1.4 kg (3 lb) sea bass, cleaned

75 ml (3 fl oz) dry white wine

lemon slices and dill sprigs, to garnish

Cooking fish in foil is a clean and easy method, and also prevents cooking smells if you are cooking indoors.

1. Work the butter with the dillweed, lemon rind and salt and pepper. Form into a roll, wrap in foil and chill 2–3 hours until firm.

2. Cut a sheet of foil large enough to enclose the fish. Place the bass in the centre.

3. Cut the flavoured butter roll into slices, peeling off the foil after cutting.

4. Place the butter slices inside the belly of the fish. Sprinkle the outside of the fish with salt and pepper, then slowly pour over the wine and lemon juice.

5. Fold the foil over the fish to form a loose package so that the wine and juices do not leak out. Place the foil package on the barbecue and grill for 45 minutes. Serve hot, straight from the foil.

Bass with Fennel

SERVES FOUR

2 bass, about 350 g (12 oz) each, cleaned and prepared

150 ml (¼ pint) dry white wine

30–45 ml (2–3 tbsp) vegetable oil

salt and freshly ground pepper

10 ml (2 tsp) lemon juice

a few sprigs of fennel

Silvery bass is not a very well known fish in Great Britain. The white, delicate flesh needs careful cooking and is best cooked whole.

1. Make 3–4 diagonal slits 5 mm (¼ inch) deep on each side of the bass.

2. Combine the wine, 15 ml (1 tbsp) oil, salt and pepper to taste and the lemon juice in a dish large enough to take the fish. Slip the fennel into the slits in the fish, then place in

the marinade. Cover and marinate in the refrigerator for at least 3 hours. Turn and baste from time to time.

3. To cook, drain the fish and brush with more oil. Cook under a preheated grill until the fish flakes when tested with a knife. The skin should show signs of bubbling. Alternatively, cook over a barbecue. Serve on a bed of lemon slices with a little hot marinade poured over.

Creamy Cod Bake

SERVES FOUR

50 g (2 oz) butter

4 cod steaks

900 g (2 lb) spinach, cooked and chopped

2.5 ml (½ level tsp) grated nutmeg

salt and freshly ground pepper

450 ml (¾ pint) Mornay Sauce (see page 90)

50 g (2 oz) Cheddar cheese, grated

A deliciously nourishing dish, particularly suitable for children. The fish is cooked on a bed of nutritious spinach. Serve with creamed potatoes and grilled or baked tomatoes.

1. Melt half the butter in a frying pan, add the cod steaks and fry for a few minutes on each side until golden.

2. Put the spinach in the base of an ovenproof dish and mix in the remaining

butter with half the nutmeg. Season.

3. Arrange the cod steaks in a single layer on top of the spinach and pour over any juices.

4. Stir the remaining nutmeg into the mornay sauce, then pour the sauce evenly over the fish. Sprinkle over the cheese.

5. Bake in the oven at 190°C (375°F) mark 5 for 30 minutes until golden and bubbling.

Steamed Mullet with Chilli Sauce

SERVES TWO

1 grey mullet, about 550 g (1¼ lb), cleaned
75 ml (5 tbsp) tomato ketchup
15 ml (1 tbsp) soy sauce
pinch of chilli powder
75 ml (5 tbsp) white wine
1 small red pepper, seeded and cut into matchsticks
1 small green pepper, seeded and cut into matchsticks
5 ml (1 level tsp) cornflour
15 ml (1 tbsp) chopped fresh parsley
salt and freshly ground pepper

Silvery grey, with dark grey lines along its flank, the grey mullet is found in coastal waters and estuaries all over the world. First marinated then steamed, this flavoursome dish is served with a hot piquant sauce.

1. Place the mullet in a shallow dish.

2. Whisk together the tomato ketchup, soy sauce, chilli powder and wine. Make three deep slashes along the length of the fish. Pour over the marinade. Cover and leave for 2 hours.

3. Drain off the marinade and reserve. Place the fish on a rack over a roasting tin half full of water. Cover tightly with foil. Steam the fish over a medium heat for 20–25 minutes. When cooked, the eyes should be white.

4. To make the chilli sauce, place the marinade and peppers in a saucepan. Stir in the cornflour mixed to a smooth paste with 15 ml (1 tbsp) water. Bring to the boil and simmer for 4–5 minutes. Stir in the parsley and salt and pepper to taste.

5. Carefully lift the steamed mullet on to a warmed serving plate. Spoon over the sauce to serve.

Red Mullet Parcels

SERVES FOUR

60 ml (4 tbsp) olive oil
60 ml (4 tbsp) dry white vermouth
2 garlic cloves, skinned and crushed
salt and freshly ground pepper
4 red mullet, about 225 g (8 oz) each, cleaned
4 rosemary sprigs
fresh rosemary sprigs and lemon slices, to garnish

The delicate flesh of the red mullet used in this recipe is more highly prized than that of the grey mullet.

1. Mix together the oil, vermouth and garlic. Add salt and pepper to taste.

2. Cut four rectangles of foil, each one large enough to enclose one red mullet. Brush with a little of the olive oil mixture.

3. Place one fish in the centre of each piece of foil and pour over the remaining olive oil mixture. Place a rosemary sprig on top of each fish.

4. Bring the long sides of the foil to meet over the fish and fold over several times to close and seal completely.

5. Fold over the ends of the foil so that the fish are completely sealed in, like parcels.

6. Put the parcels in a single layer in a baking tin and bake in the oven at 180°C (350°F) mark 4 for 20 minutes or until tender.

7. Remove the fish carefully from the parcels and place on a warmed serving dish. Pour over the juices that have collected on the foil. Garnish each fish with a fresh rosemary sprig and a slice of lemon and serve immediately.

Stuffed Cod Crêpes

SERVES SIX

175 g (6 oz) plain flour, plus 45 ml (3 tbsp)
50 g (2 oz) salted peanuts, very finely chopped
2 eggs
15 ml (1 tbsp) vegetable oil
450 ml (¾ pint) milk and water mixed
700 g (1½ lb) cod fillet
568 ml (1 pint) milk
50 g (2 oz) butter
100 g (4 oz) celery, chopped
5 ml (1 level tsp) curry powder
salt and freshly ground pepper
75 ml (5 tbsp) single cream
50 g (2 oz) Cheddar cheese, grated
chopped fresh parsley, to garnish

These lightly curried fish pancakes would make a substantial starter as well as a satisfying supper dish. The crêpe batter has chopped nuts added to it; make sure they are finely chopped otherwise the texture of the crêpes may be spoilt.

1. Make the batter for the crêpes. Whisk 175 g (6 oz) flour, the chopped peanuts, eggs, oil and half the milk and water mixture until quite smooth. Whisk in the remaining liquid.

2. Lightly oil an 18 cm (7 inch) heavy frying pan. Spoon in about 30 ml (2 tbsp) batter, tipping the pan to spread the batter. Cook until golden underneath, then turn over and cook the other side. Make twelve pancakes in total, keep covered.

3. Place the cod in a deep frying pan with the milk. Cover and poach gently for about 12 minutes until the fish is tender and begins to flake. Strain off and reserve the liquid. Flake the fish, discarding skin and bone.

4. Melt the butter in a heavy-based saucepan, add the celery and curry powder and fry gently for 1 minute, stirring. Remove from the heat and stir in the remaining flour, reserved liquid from cooking the fish and salt and pepper to taste. Bring to the boil, stirring, and simmer for 1 minute. Remove from the heat and fold in the cream and flaked fish.

5. Divide the filling between the crêpes, roll up and place side by side in a single layer in a greased shallow ovenproof dish. Sprinkle the grated cheese over the top and cover loosely with foil.

6. Bake in the oven at 180°C (350°F) mark 4 for about 40 minutes. Garnish.

Spanish Cod with Peppers, Tomatoes and Garlic

SERVES FOUR

700 g (1½ lb) cod fillet, skinned
1 litre (1¾ pints) mussels or about 450 g (1 lb) weight, cooked (see page 98)
30 ml (2 tbsp) vegetable oil
2 medium onions, skinned and sliced
1 red pepper, cored, seeded and sliced
1 green pepper, cored, seeded and sliced
1–2 garlic cloves, skinned and crushed
450 g (1 lb) tomatoes, skinned and chopped
300 ml (½ pint) white wine
2.5 ml (½ tsp) Tabasco sauce, or to taste
1 bay leaf
salt and freshly ground pepper

Mussels are at their best during the colder months, from October to March. Serve this colourful dish with hot crusty bread, followed by a crisp green salad.

1. Cut the cod into chunks. Shell all but four mussels.

2. Heat the oil in a frying pan, add the onions, peppers and garlic and cook for about 5 minutes until starting to soften. Add the tomatoes and half the wine, bring to the boil and simmer for 5 minutes, then add the Tabasco.

3. Layer the fish and vegetables in a casserole and add the bay leaf and salt and pepper to taste.

4. Pour over the remaining wine. Push the four mussels in shells into the top layer. Cover and cook in the oven at 180°C (350°F) mark 4 for 1 hour. Discard the bay leaf. Serve hot.

Opposite: Hot Fish Terrine with Gruyère Sauce (see page 24)

Coley and Potato Pie

SERVES SIX

1.4 kg (3 lb) potatoes, peeled and cut into large pieces
salt and freshly ground pepper
900 g (2 lb) coley fillet, skinned
15 ml (1 tbsp) vegetable oil
50 g (2 oz) butter
1 medium onion, skinned and thinly sliced
5 ml (1 level tsp) mixed dried herbs
45 ml (3 level tbsp) plain flour
400 g (14 oz) can tomatoes
30 ml (2 tbsp) capers
1 garlic clove, skinned and crushed
150 ml ($\frac{1}{4}$ pint) milk
600 ml (1 pint) natural yogurt
2 eggs, beaten

An economical family fish pie moistened with a delicious and healthy yogurt sauce. Coley, a member of the cod family, is one of the cheapest fish to buy. Although on the slab it looks an off-putting pinkish-grey, when cooked it becomes an appetising creamy white.

1. Put the potatoes in a saucepan and cover with cold, salted water. Bring to the boil and simmer for 10 minutes. Drain well. Cool and slice thinly.

2. Chop the coley into 2.5 cm (1 inch) pieces.

3. Heat the oil and 25 g (1 oz) of the butter in a pan, add the onion and fry for 4–5 minutes until soft.

4. Stir in the mixed herbs and 15 ml (1 tbsp) of the flour. Cook, stirring, for 1–2 minutes before adding the tomatoes, fish and capers.

Bring to the boil and simmer for 1 minute until thickened. Add salt and pepper to taste and remove from the heat.

5. Melt the remaining butter in a saucepan with the garlic. Add the remaining flour and cook gently, stirring, for 1–2 minutes. Remove from the heat and gradually blend in the milk. Bring to the boil, stirring constantly, then simmer for 2–3 minutes. Remove from the heat and beat in the yogurt and eggs.

6. In a shallow 3.4 litre (6 pint) ovenproof dish, layer the sliced potatoes with the fish and tomato mixture, finishing with a layer of potato.

7. Spoon the yogurt sauce evenly over the potatoes. Bake in the oven at 190°C (375°F) mark 5 for about 40 minutes. Brown the top under a preheated grill before serving.

Seafood Stir-fry

SERVES FOUR

2 celery sticks, trimmed
1 medium carrot, peeled
350 g (12 oz) coley fillet, skinned and boned
350 g (12 oz) Iceberg or Cos lettuce
about 45 ml (3 tbsp) peanut oil
1 garlic clove, skinned and crushed
100 g (4 oz) peeled prawns
425 g (15 oz) can whole baby sweetcorn, drained
5 ml (1 tsp) anchovy essence
salt and freshly ground pepper

Stir-frying is a Chinese method of cooking which is extremely quick, preserving vitamins and preventing the ingredients from soaking up too much oil. When stir-frying lettuce, always use one of the crisp varieties for a fresh, crunchy result.

1. Slice the celery and carrot into thin matchsticks, 5 cm (2 inches) long. Cut the fish into 2.5 cm (1 inch) chunks.

2. Shred the lettuce finely with a sharp knife, discarding the core and any thick stalks.

3. Heat 15 ml (1 tbsp) of the oil in a wok or large frying pan until smoking. Add the lettuce and fry for about 30 seconds until

lightly cooked. Transfer to a serving dish with a slotted spoon and keep warm in a low oven, while completing the stir-fry.

4. Heat another 30 ml (2 tbsp) of oil in the pan until smoking. Add the celery, carrot, coley and garlic and stir-fry over high heat for 2–3 minutes, adding more oil if necessary.

5. Lower the heat, add the prawns, baby sweetcorn and anchovy essence. Toss well together for 2–3 minutes to heat through and coat all the ingredients in the sauce (the fish will flake apart).

6. Add salt and pepper to taste, spoon on top of the lettuce and serve immediately.

Opposite: Skate with Capers and Black Butter (see page 30)

Dover Sole au Basilic

SERVES FOUR

4 Dover sole, about 400 g (14 oz) each, skinned and cut diagonally across the head (see page 96)
salt and freshly ground pepper
25 g (1 oz) butter
120 ml (4 fl oz) dry white wine
600 ml (1 pint) Tomato Sauce with 10 ml (2 tsp) chopped fresh basil (see page 90)
50 g (2 oz) tomato, skinned, seeded and chopped

Dover sole here is baked in the oven with white wine, then served with a tomato sauce flavoured with basil. The perfect herb accompaniment to tomato, basil has a warm, pungent fragrance.

1. Sprinkle the sole with salt and pepper. Butter two ovenproof dishes and lay the fish on them—two to a dish, head to tail. Add the wine, then cover with buttered greaseproof paper or foil.

2. Cook in the oven at 200°C (400°F) mark 6 for about 10 minutes, avoiding over-cooking. Remove the fish and drain well. (Keep whole or fillet, as liked.)

3. Lightly coat the base of a warmed oval platter or four oval plates with half of the hot tomato sauce and lay the fish on top.

4. Add the chopped tomato to the remaining sauce and use to coat the fish.

Dover Sole Florentine

SERVES FOUR

4 Dover sole, about 400 g (14 oz) each, skinned and cut diagonally across the head (see page 96)
salt and freshly ground pepper
50 g (2 oz) butter
300 ml (½ pint) Fish Stock (see page 88)
450 g (1 lb) cooked spinach
600 ml (1 pint) Mornay Sauce (see page 90)
50 g (2 oz) Cheddar cheese, grated

Before cooking spinach, wash well as it can be gritty. Rich in iron, spinach can then be cooked using only the water still clinging to the leaves after washing.

1. Sprinkle the sole with salt and pepper. Butter two ovenproof dishes and lay the fish on them—two to a dish, head to tail. Add the fish stock, then cover with buttered greaseproof paper or foil. Cook in the oven at 200°C (400°F) mark 6 for about 10 minutes.

2. Melt the remaining butter in a frying pan, add the spinach and reheat. Place the spinach on a warmed platter and keep hot.

3. Remove the fish and drain. (Keep whole or fillet, as liked.) Lay the fish on top of the spinach.

4. Coat the fish with mornay sauce. Sprinkle with the grated cheese and place under a preheated grill until bubbling.

Goujons of Dover Sole

SERVES FOUR

about 800 g (1¾ lb) Dover sole fillets, skinned
salt and freshly ground pepper
about 100 g (4 oz) plain flour
3 eggs, beaten, with 45 ml (3 tbsp) milk
225 g (8 oz) fresh breadcrumbs
vegetable oil, for deep frying
lemon slices and parsley sprigs, to garnish
1 quantity Tartare Sauce, to serve (see page 90)

Goujons are small strips of fish coated in egg and breadcrumbs, then deep fried. The parsley garnish can be deep fried too—simply wash and thoroughly dry parsley sprigs then deep fry for a few seconds until crisp and green!

1. Cut the sole fillets into strips about 7.5 × 1 cm (3 × ½ inch). Sprinkle the fish strips with salt and pepper and roll in the flour. Shake well to remove excess, dip into the egg mixture, then the breadcrumbs.

2. Roll the goujons on the flat surface to remove excess crumbs and to ensure a good shape.

3. Cook the goujons in batches in a deep-fat fryer at 185°C (360°F) for about 3 minutes until golden brown. Drain well.

4. Serve on a warmed oval plate, garnished with lemon slices and parsley. Hand tartare sauce separately.

Dover Sole Cubat

SERVES FOUR

4 Dover sole, about 400 g (14 oz) each, skinned and cut diagonally across the head (see page 96)

salt and freshly ground pepper

225 ml (8 fl oz) dry white wine

50 g (2 oz) butter

15 g (½ oz) shallot or onion, skinned and finely chopped

450 g (1 lb) mushrooms, wiped and finely chopped

25 g (1 oz) chopped fresh parsley

600 ml (1 pint) Mornay Sauce (see page 90)

about 50 ml (2 fl oz) Hollandaise Sauce (see page 90)

Served on a bed of finely chopped mushrooms, Dover Sole Cubat is coated with an enriched Mornay sauce. Serve with a green vegetable, such as broccoli.

1. Sprinkle the sole with salt and pepper. Butter two ovenproof dishes and lay the fish on them—two to a dish, head to tail. Add the wine, then cover with buttered greaseproof paper or foil.

2. Cook in the oven at 200°C (400°F) mark 6 for about 10 minutes, avoiding overcooking.

3. Melt the remaining butter in a pan, add the shallot and gently fry until soft, without colouring. Add the mushrooms and cook slowly until the mixture is fairly dry. Add salt and pepper to taste and sprinkle over the chopped parsley.

4. Remove the fish and drain, reserving the cooking liquid. (Keep whole or fillet, as liked.)

5. Boil the cooking liquid to reduce by half, add the mornay sauce and reboil. Remove from heat and add the Hollandaise sauce. Do not reboil.

6. Spread the mushroom mixture on to the base of a warmed oval ovenproof platter. Lay the fish on top and coat with the sauce. Glaze under a preheated grill for 1–2 minutes. Serve immediately.

Dover Sole Hélène

SERVES FOUR

4 Dover sole, about 400 g (14 oz) each, skinned and cut diagonally across the head (see page 96)

salt and freshly ground pepper

75 g (3 oz) butter

600 ml (1 pint) Fish Stock (see page 88)

350 g (12 oz) green noodles

good pinch of oregano

50 ml (2 fl oz) double cream

600 ml (1 pint) Mornay Sauce (see page 90)

1 quantity of Hollandaise Sauce (see page 90)

Served with a rich and creamy cheese sauce and placed on a bed of green noodles, this luxury sole recipe needs only a tossed green salad to complete the dish.

1. Sprinkle the sole with salt and pepper. Butter two ovenproof dishes and lay the fish on them—two to a dish, head to tail. Add the fish stock and cover with buttered greaseproof paper or foil.

2. Cook in the oven at 180°C (350°F) mark 4 for about 10 minutes, avoiding overcooking.

3. Meanwhile, bring a large saucepan of water to the boil. Add the noodles and cook until just tender. Drain and rinse in cold water to refresh. Drain again. Melt the butter in the saucepan, add the noodles and gently reheat. Add salt, pepper and oregano to taste.

Transfer to a warmed serving dish and keep hot.

4. When cooked, drain the fish well. (Keep the fish whole or fillet, as liked.)

5. Whip the cream and add to the mornay sauce with the Hollandaise. Lightly coat warmed heatproof plates with the sauce, place the fish or fillets on top and coat with the remaining sauce. Lightly brown under a preheated grill, then serve immediately with the noodles.

Dover Sole Dugléré

SERVES FOUR

4 Dover sole, about 400 g (14 oz) each, skinned and cut diagonally across the head (see page 96)
salt and freshly ground pepper
100 g (4 oz) butter
50 g (2 oz) shallot or onion, skinned and finely chopped
4 medium tomatoes, skinned, seeded and roughly chopped
120 ml (4 fl oz) dry white wine
120 ml (4 fl oz) Fish Stock (see page 88)
120 ml (4 fl oz) Fish Velouté (see page 89)
juice of ½ lemon
7.5 ml (½ tbsp) chopped fresh parsley

This dish is named after a famous 18th century French chef: à la Dugléré refers to a method of cooking white fish in white wine with shallots and tomatoes.

1. Sprinkle the sole with salt and pepper. Butter two ovenproof dishes and lay the fish on them—two to a dish, head to tail. Sprinkle the fish with the shallot, tomatoes, white wine and fish stock. Cover with buttered greaseproof paper or foil.

2. Poach in the oven at 200°C (400°F) mark 6 for about 10 minutes, avoiding overcooking. When cooked, remove and drain, reserving the cooking liquid. (Keep the fish whole or fillet, as liked.)

3. Boil the cooking liquid to reduce by half, add the velouté and reboil. Strain, retaining the tomato, and add the lemon juice and salt and pepper to taste. Add the remaining butter to the sauce, stirring in until glossy. Stir in the chopped parsley.

4. Put a little of the sauce on to a warmed oval platter. Lay the fish on top, coat with the remaining sauce and serve immediately.

Dover Sole Meunière

SERVES FOUR

4 Dover sole, about 400 g (14 oz) each, skinned and cut diagonally across the head (see page 96)
salt and freshly ground pepper
plain flour
120 ml (4 fl oz) vegetable oil
100 g (4 oz) clarified butter (see page 91)
175 g (6 oz) butter
juice of 2 lemons
skinned lemon slices and chopped fresh parsley, to garnish

The traditional way of cooking Dover Sole—on the bone—is best. However, sole fillets can be cooked this way too. This classic recipe brings out the incomparable and exquisite flavour for which Dover sole is so famous.

1. Sprinkle the sole with salt and pepper. Coat with the flour, shaking well to remove excess.

2. Heat the oil and clarified butter in two very large or oval frying pans. When hot, add the fish, presentation side down—two fish to a pan if possible, head to tail. Cook gently for about 5 minutes, then turn over and cook on the other side for about the same length of time. Transfer the fish to a warmed oval platter.

3. Heat a small saucepan and drop in the 175 g (6 oz) butter. Shake the pan. The butter will sizzle and melt quickly, turning a golden brown colour, and giving off a 'nutty' aroma. Add the lemon juice to the butter and pour immediately over the fish through a fine sieve.

4. Garnish with lemon slices along the back of the fish and sprinkle with chopped parsley.

Ceviche

SERVES FOUR

450 g (1 lb) haddock fillets, skinned
5 ml (1 tsp) coriander seeds
5 ml (1 tsp) black peppercorns
juice of 6 limes
5 ml (1 level tsp) salt
30 ml (2 tbsp) olive oil
bunch of spring onions, trimmed and sliced
4 tomatoes, skinned and chopped
dash of Tabasco, or to taste
30 ml (2 tbsp) chopped fresh coriander
1 avocado, to finish
lime slices and fresh coriander, to garnish

A tangy fish dish with a difference as the haddock is marinated in lime juice and cooking is not needed. Limes are expensive and not always available, but they are worth the effort of trying to get hold of.

1. Cut the haddock fillets diagonally into thin, even strips and place in a bowl.

2. Crush the coriander seeds and peppercorns to a fine powder in a mortar and pestle. Mix with the lime juice and salt, then pour over the fish. Cover and chill for 24 hours, turning the fish occasionally.

3. The next day, heat the oil in a pan, add the spring onions and fry gently for 5 minutes. Add the tomatoes and Tabasco to taste and toss together over a brisk heat for 1–2 minutes. Remove from the heat and leave to cool for 20–30 minutes.

4. To serve, drain the fish from the marinade, discarding the marinade. Combine the fish with the spring onion and tomatoes and the chopped coriander. Taste and adjust seasoning, if necessary.

5. Halve the avocado, peel and remove the stone. Slice the flesh crossways. Arrange the slices around the inside of a serving bowl and pile the ceviche in the centre. Garnish with lime slices and coriander leaves. Serve chilled.

Fresh Haddock Mousse

SERVES SIX

350 g (12 oz) haddock fillet
200 ml (7 fl oz) milk
1 bay leaf
6 peppercorns
salt and freshly ground pepper
7.5 ml (1½ level tsp) powdered gelatine
25 g (1 oz) butter
30 ml (2 level tbsp) plain flour
15 ml (1 tbsp) Dijon mustard
30 ml (2 tbsp) tomato ketchup
5 ml (1 tsp) Worcestershire sauce
90 ml (6 tbsp) double cream
150 ml (¼ pint) Mayonnaise (see page 91)
15 ml (1 tbsp) lemon juice
watercress sprigs, to garnish

Excess chilling takes the edge off the delicate flavour of this fish so don't serve straight from the refrigerator. And the texture is not as light if left overnight.

1. Put the haddock in a sauté or frying pan. Pour over the milk and add the bay leaf and peppercorns with a good pinch of salt. Bring slowly to the boil, cover and simmer for 5–10 minutes or until the fish flakes easily when tested with a fork.

2. Meanwhile, place 30 ml (2 tbsp) very hot water in a small bowl and sprinkle in the gelatine. Stir briskly until dissolved. Leave to cool. Strain the liquor from the fish and reserve. Skin and flake the fish, discarding any bones.

3. Melt the butter in a medium saucepan, add the flour and cook gently, stirring, for 1–2 minutes. Remove from the heat and gradually blend in the fish juices. Bring to the boil, stirring constantly, then simmer for 3 minutes until thickened and smooth. Remove from the heat and stir in the soaked gelatine.

4. Mix the sauce, fish, mustard, tomato ketchup, Worcestershire sauce, salt and pepper in a blender or food processor until just smooth. Turn out into a bowl and cool. Lightly whip the cream.

5. Lastly, stir in the mayonnaise and lemon juice with cream. Adjust the seasoning and spoon into six individual soufflé or ramekin dishes; refrigerate to set.

6. When firm, cover with cling film. Allow to come to at room temperature for 30 minutes before serving. Garnish with watercress sprigs and serve with crusty rolls.

Haddock and Mushroom Puffs

SERVES FOUR

½ quantity Puff Pastry (see page 92)
450 g (1 lb) haddock fillet, skinned
215 g (7½ oz) can creamed mushrooms
5 ml (1 tsp) lemon juice
20 ml (4 tsp) capers, chopped
15 ml (1 tbsp) snipped fresh chives or 5 ml (1 tsp) dried
salt and freshly ground pepper
1 egg

Simply serve this substantial lunch or supper dish with a green vegetable such as French beans. To make pastry leaves, roll out the trimmings thinly into 2.5 cm (1 inch) wide strips. Cut into diamond shapes and mark the veins of the leaves with the back of a knife.

1. Roll out the pastry on a floured surface into a 40 cm (16 inch) square. Using a sharp knife, cut into four squares, trim the edges and reserve the trimmings of pastry.

2. Place the squares on dampened baking sheets. Divide the haddock into four and place diagonally across the pastry squares.

3. Combine the creamed mushrooms with the lemon juice, capers, chives and salt and pepper to taste. Mix well, then spoon over the pieces of haddock fillet.

4. Brush the edges of each square lightly with water. Bring the four points of each square together and seal the edges to form an envelope-shaped parcel,

5. Decorate with pastry leaves and make a small hole in the centre of each parcel. Chill for 30 minutes.

6. Beat the egg with a pinch of salt and use to glaze the pastry. Bake in the oven at 220°C (425°F) mark 7 for about 20 minutes or until the pastry is golden brown and well risen. Serve hot.

Haddock and Prawn Gratinée

SERVES EIGHT

450 g (1 lb) haddock fillet, skinned
25 g (1 oz) butter
1 medium onion, skinned and finely chopped
30 ml (2 tbsp) plain flour
300 ml (½ pint) milk
30 ml (2 tbsp) dry white wine
175 g (6 oz) peeled prawns
75 g (3 oz) Gruyère or mature Cheddar cheese, grated
salt and freshly ground pepper
chopped fresh parsley, to garnish

Haddock, with its mild flavour and fairly firm texture, is a good choice for this dinner party starter. Serve with French bread and a chilled dry white wine.

1. Cut the haddock fillet into 16 small strips. Fold the strips in half and place two each in eight individual ramekin or gratin dishes.

2. Melt the butter in a saucepan, add the onion and fry gently until soft. Add the flour and cook gently, stirring, for 1–2 minutes. Remove from the heat and gradually blend in the milk and wine. Bring to the boil, stirring constantly, then simmer for 3 minutes.

3. Remove the sauce from the heat, add the prawns and 50 g (2 oz) of the cheese with salt and pepper to taste.

4. Spoon a little sauce into each ramekin, to cover the fish. Sprinkle the remaining cheese on top.

5. Bake in the oven at 190°C (375°F) mark 5 for 30 minutes. Serve immediately, garnished with chopped parsley.

Creamy Fish Casserole

SERVES FOUR TO SIX

700 g (1½ lb) hake, skinned and cut into bite-sized pieces
30 ml (2 level tbsp) plain flour
salt and freshly ground pepper
40 g (1½ oz) butter
15 ml (1 tbsp) vegetable oil
600 ml (1 pint) dry cider
2 bay leaves, crumbled
900 g (2 lb) old floury potatoes, scrubbed
150 ml (¼ pint) single cream
30 ml (2 tbsp) chopped fresh parsley

This layered casserole needs no other accompaniment than a seasonal green vegetable. If liked, serve ice cold dry cider with the meal.

1. Coat the pieces of hake in the flour seasoned with salt and pepper to taste.

2. Melt 25 g (1 oz) of the butter with the oil in a frying pan, add the pieces of hake and fry gently until golden on all sides. Remove from the pan with a slotted spoon and set aside.

3. Pour the cider into the frying pan and stir to dislodge the sediment from the bottom and sides of the pan. Add the bay leaves and salt and pepper. Bring to the boil and simmer for a few minutes, then pour into a jug.

4. Blanch the potatoes in their skins in boiling salted water for 10 minutes. Drain, leave until cool enough to handle, then peel off the skins and slice.

5. Put half the fish in the bottom of a shallow casserole. Stir the cream into the cider mixture, then pour half over the fish.

6. Cover with half the potato slices, overlapping them so that they cover the fish completely. Sprinkle with half the parsley. Put the remaining fish on top of the potatoes, then pour over the remaining cider and cream.

7. Cover with the remaining potato slices as before, then dot with the remaining butter. Cook in the oven at 190°C (375°F) mark 5 for 45 minutes. Sprinkle the remaining parsley over the top before serving.

Cannelloni with Spinach

SERVES SIX

200 g (7 oz) cannelloni (18 tubes)
salt and freshly ground pepper
30 ml (2 tbsp) vegetable oil
700 g (1½ lb) hake fillets, skinned
75 g (3 oz) fresh white breadcrumbs
4 eggs, beaten
900 g (2 lb) spinach, cooked and finely chopped
25 g (1 oz) butter
25 g (1 oz) plain flour
450 ml (¾ pint) milk
pinch of grated nutmeg

Hake and spinach provide an unusual filling for cannelloni tubes in this satisfying pasta dish. Hake is a member of the cod family and is found in deep seas in most parts of the world. It has a slightly firmer flesh than cod, and makes a pleasing change.

1. Cook the cannelloni in a large saucepan of boiling, salted water with the oil for about 10 minutes. Drain well. Keep under cold water until required.

2. Finely chop the hake. Beat 50 g (2 oz) of the breadcrumbs and the fish together in a large bowl. Gradually mix in the eggs, beating well between each addition. Stir 225 g (8 oz) of the spinach into the fish mixture. Add salt and pepper to taste.

3. Drain the cannelloni. Spoon some of the mixture carefully into each tube. Place in a shallow ovenproof dish.

4. Melt the butter in a saucepan, add the flour and cook gently, stirring, for 1–2 minutes. Remove from the heat and gradually blend in the milk. Bring to the boil, stirring constantly, then simmer for 3 minutes until thickened and smooth. Stir in the remaining spinach, nutmeg and seasoning. Spoon over the filled cannelloni and sprinkle with remaining breadcrumbs.

5. Bake in the oven at 200°C (400°F) mark 6 for about 40 minutes.

Hot Fish Terrine with Gruyère Sauce

SERVES SIX

75 g (3 oz) butter
1 garlic clove, skinned and crushed
60 ml (4 level tbsp) plain flour
750 ml (1¼ pints) milk
550 g (1¼ lb) hake fillets, skinned and chopped
150 ml (¼ pint) double cream
10 ml (2 tsp) anchovy essence
3 eggs
1 egg yolk
salt and freshly ground pepper
30 ml (2 tbsp) chopped fresh parsley
100 g (4 oz) peeled prawns, chopped
100 g (4 oz) Gruyère cheese, grated
watercress sprigs and 6 whole prawns, to garnish

An unusual rich, light-textured fish terrine with a centre layer of prawns, accompanied by a Gruyère cheese and prawn sauce.

1. Lightly butter and base line a 1.6 litre (2¾ pint) shallow loaf tin or terrine.

2. Melt 40 g (1½ oz) of the butter in a saucepan. Add the garlic. Stir in 45 ml (3 tbsp) of the flour and cook gently, stirring, for 1–2 minutes. Remove from the heat and gradually blend in 450 ml (¾ pint) of the milk. Bring to the boil, stirring constantly, then simmer for 2 minutes until thickened.

3. In a blender or food processor, purée the sauce, raw chopped hake, cream, anchovy essence, eggs and yolk. Season lightly.

4. Spoon half the fish mixture into the tin. Sprinkle with parsley and half the prawns. Spoon in the rest of fish mixture. Cover tightly with buttered greaseproof paper.

5. Place in a roasting tin with hot water to come halfway up the sides of the terrine. Cook in the oven at 150°C (300°F) mark 2 for about 1¾ hours.

6. Just before the terrine is cooked, make the sauce. Melt 25 g (1 oz) butter in a saucepan, add the remaining flour and cook gently, stirring for 1–2 minutes. Remove from the heat and gradually blend in the remaining milk. Bring to the boil, stirring constantly, then simmer for 2 minutes until thickened and smooth. Remove from the heat, stir in the grated cheese and remaining prawns. Add salt and pepper to taste.

7. Invert the terrine on to a warmed serving dish and tilt slightly to drain off the juices. Remove the cooking container. Spoon a little sauce over the terrine and garnish with watercress and prawns. Serve the remaining sauce separately.

Seafood Tart

SERVES FOUR

175 g (6 oz) Shortcrust Pastry (see page 93), made using 45 ml (3 tbsp) toasted sesame seeds
225 g (8 oz) hake fillet, skinned
150 ml (¼ pint) milk
1 bay leaf
25 g (1 oz) butter
30 ml (2 level tbsp) plain flour
1 egg, beaten
1 egg, hard-boiled and roughly chopped
50 g (2 oz) peeled prawns
salt and freshly ground pepper
15 ml (1 tbsp) French mustard

Sesame seeds, which are rich in protein, potassium, calcium and vitamin B, make an unusual but healthy addition to the pastry base of this tart. To toast sesame seeds, cook in a dry frying pan over a medium heat until golden.

1. Add the sesame seeds to the flour and make up the pastry. Roll out the pastry and use to line a 20.5 cm (8 inch) plain flan ring on a baking sheet. Chill for 10–15 minutes. Bake blind in the oven at 190°C (375°F) mark 5 until set but not browned.

2. Put the hake, milk and bay leaf in a saucepan and poach for about 10 minutes. Strain off the milk and reserve. Flake the fish.

3. Melt the butter in a saucepan, add the flour and cook gently, stirring, for 1–2 minutes. Remove from the heat and gradually blend in the reserved milk. Bring to the boil, stirring constantly, then simmer for 3 minutes until thick and smooth. Remove from the heat, stir in the beaten egg, hard-boiled egg, flaked fish and prawns. Add salt and pepper to taste.

4. Spread the mustard in the flan. Pour in the sauce mixture. Return to the oven for 25–30 minutes. Serve warm.

Summer Fish Hot Pot

SERVES FOUR

50 g (2 oz) butter
4 sticks of celery, trimmed and finely sliced
50 g (2 oz) plain flour
450 ml (¾ pint) milk
salt and fresh ground pepper
700 g (1½ lb) hake fillet
275 g (10 oz) Florence fennel, untrimmed weight
60 ml (4 tbsp) chopped fresh parsley
10 ml (2 tsp) lemon juice
450 g (1 lb) new potatoes, boiled and sliced
chopped fresh parsley, to garnish

This Mediterranean-style fish stew contains fennel and potatoes, and so does not need another vegetable dish. Fennel is a bulbous-looking vegetable, similar in texture to celery but with a distinctive aniseed flavour which mellows during cooking.

1. Melt the butter in a flameproof casserole, add the celery and cook gently for 5 minutes until soft. Add the flour and cook gently, stirring, for 1–2 minutes. Remove from the heat and gradually blend in the milk. Bring to the boil, stirring constantly, then simmer for 3 minutes. Add salt and pepper to taste and remove from the heat.

2. Place the hake in a saucepan and just cover with water. Bring to the boil, remove from the heat and drain. Cut into fork-size pieces, discarding the skin and any bones.

3. Trim the fennel and cut into thin slices. Blanch in boiling salted water for 2 minutes and drain.

4. Add the fennel, parsley and lemon juice to the sauce; mix well. Stir in the fish, taking care not to break up the flesh; cool for 30 minutes.

5. Arrange the potato slices on top of the fish. Cover the dish with buttered foil. Bake in the oven at 180°C (350°F) mark 4 for about 50 minutes or until the fish is cooked. Sprinkle with chopped parsley before serving.

Indonesian Fish Curry

SERVES FOUR

1 small onion, skinned and chopped
1 garlic clove, skinned and chopped
2.5 cm (1 inch) piece fresh root ginger, skinned and chopped
5 ml (1 level tsp) turmeric
2.5 ml (½ level tsp) laos powder
1.25 ml (¼ level tsp) chilli powder
30 ml (2 tbsp) vegetable oil
salt
700 g (1½ lb) hake fillets, skinned and cut into bite-sized pieces
225 g (8 oz) peeled prawns
300 ml (½ pint) coconut milk
juice of 1 lime
shredded coconut and lime wedges, to garnish

Serve this white fish and prawn curry with plain boiled rice, prawn crackers and lime pickle. Laos powder, with its peppery hot taste, is used extensively in the cooking of Southeast Asia; it comes from a root rather like ginger. Look for it in specialist delicatessens in small bottles, sometimes labelled galangal or galingale.

To make up the coconut milk, break half a 198 g (7 oz) packet of creamed coconut into a bowl. Add 300 ml (½ pint) warm water and stir until dissolved.

1. Work the onion, garlic, ginger, turmeric, laos powder, chilli powder and oil in a blender or food processor with 2.5 ml (½ tsp) salt. Transfer the mixture to a flameproof casserole and fry gently, stirring, for 5 minutes. Add the hake pieces and prawns and fry for a few minutes more, tossing the fish to coat with the spice mixture.

2. Add the coconut milk, shake the pan and turn the fish gently in the liquid. (Take care not to break up the pieces of fish.) Bring slowly to boiling point, then lower the heat, cover and simmer for 10 minutes until tender.

3. Add the lime juice, taste and adjust seasoning, then transfer to a warmed serving dish and sprinkle with coconut. Serve hot, garnished with lime wedges.

Fricassée of Halibut with Coriander

SERVES SIX

700 g (1½ lb) halibut cutlets, skinned and boned

450 g (1 lb) monkfish fillet, skinned and boned

150 ml (¼ pint) dry vermouth

1 small onion, skinned and sliced

salt and freshly ground pepper

100 g (4 oz) small button mushrooms, wiped

40 g (1½ oz) butter

45 ml (3 level tbsp) plain flour

30 ml (2 tbsp) chopped fresh coriander

60 ml (4 tbsp) single cream

coriander sprigs, to garnish

Halibut is the largest of the flat fish, with firm, milky white flesh that doesn't fall apart during cooking. Delicately scented coriander is the herb used to flavour this dish.

1. Cut the fish into large, fork-sized pieces. Place in a medium saucepan, cover with cold water and bring slowly to the boil. Strain the fish in a colander and then rinse off any scum.

2. Return the fish to the clean pan and pour over the vermouth and 300 ml (½ pint) water. Add the onion and salt and pepper, then bring to the boil. Cover the pan and reduce the heat. Simmer gently for 8–10 minutes, or until the fish is just beginning to flake, adding the mushrooms after 6 minutes of the

cooking time. Strain off the cooking liquor and reserve for the sauce.

3. Melt the butter in a separate saucepan, add the flour and cook gently, stirring for 1–2 minutes. Remove from the heat and gradually blend in the cooking liquid. Bring to the boil, stirring constantly, then simmer for 2 minutes until thickened and smooth.

4. Stir in the coriander, cream, mushrooms, onion and fish and adjust the seasoning. Warm through gently, being careful not to break up the fish. Serve hot, garnished with coriander sprigs.

Monkfish Medallions

SERVES FOUR

about 900 g (2 lb) monkfish fillets, skinned

25 g (1 oz) butter

25 g (1 oz) shallot or onion, skinned and finely chopped

25 g (1 oz) green peppercorns, crushed

25 ml (1 fl oz) brandy

50 ml (2 fl oz) dry white wine

175 ml (6 fl oz) Fish Velouté (see page 89)

175 ml (6 fl oz) cream

salt and freshly ground pepper

50 g (2 oz) plain flour

75 g (3 oz) clarified butter (see page 91)

7.5 ml (½ tbsp) chopped fresh parsley

Most good fishmongers stock monkfish nowadays, although it hasn't always been a popular fish because of its ugly appearance. Even now, monkfish is almost always displayed without the head, the ugliest part. Serve these fried medallions of monkfish in creamy sauce with rice.

1. Cut the monkfish into medallions across the fillet.

2. Melt the butter in a frying pan, add the shallot and gently fry without colouring. Add the peppercorns and brandy and simmer to burn off the alcohol. Stir in the wine and simmer to reduce slightly. Add the fish velouté, reboil and add the cream. Strain and keep hot.

3. Sprinkle the monkfish with salt and pepper, dip in the flour and shake to remove

excess. Heat the clarified butter in a frying pan, add the monkfish medallions and shallow fry, without colouring, keeping the fish slightly underdone.

4. Add the fish to the sauce, simmer for a few minutes then add the chopped parsley. Serve on a warmed oval plate.

Seafood and Walnut Noodles

SERVES FOUR

450 g (1 lb) monkfish fillet, skinned
450 g (1 lb) fresh tagliatelle or 350 g (12 oz) dried
salt and freshly ground pepper
30 ml (2 tbsp) vegetable oil
25 g (1 oz) butter
100 g (4 oz) peeled prawns
50 g (2 oz) walnut pieces, roughly chopped
60 ml (4 tbsp) chopped fresh parsley
45 ml (3 tbsp) grated Parmesan cheese

White fish and shellfish combine to make a delicious ribbon noodle pasta dish, with added crunch from the walnuts. Fresh pasta is now widely available in supermarkets and is far superior to the dried kind.

1. Cut the monkfish into 2.5 cm (1 inch) pieces.

2. Cook the fresh pasta in a large saucepan of boiling, salted water with 15 ml (1 tbsp) of the oil for about 3 minutes, or the dried for 10–12 minutes.

3. Meanwhile, heat the butter with the remaining oil in a large frying pan. Add the monkfish, prawns and walnuts and fry for 3–4 minutes or until the monkfish is tender. Stir gently to prevent the fish sticking to the pan. Stir in the parsley and Parmesan. Add salt and pepper to taste.

4. Drain the tagliatelle. Season with plenty of pepper. Transfer to a warmed serving dish. Spoon the seafood mixture on top and serve.

Goujons of Monkfish

SERVES FOUR

800 g (1¾ lb) monkfish fillet, skinned
salt and freshly ground pepper
100 g (4 oz) plain flour
3 eggs, beaten with 45 ml (3 tbsp) milk
225 g (8 oz) fresh breadcrumbs
vegetable oil, for deep frying
lemon slices, parsley sprigs and slices of pickled cucumber, to garnish

Monkfish tastes very like lobster and scampi, but at a fraction of the price. Its firm, meaty flesh has always been popular in Mediterranean countries, particularly Spain and France.

1. Cut the monkfish into strips about 7.5 × 1 cm (3 × ½ inch). Sprinkle the fish strips with salt and pepper and roll in the flour. Shake well to remove the excess, then dip in egg and milk mixture and finally in the

breadcrumbs. Roll the goujons on a flat surface to remove excess crumbs and to ensure a good shape.

2. Cook the goujons in a deep-fat fryer at 185°C (360°F) for about 3–4 minutes until golden brown. Drain well.

3. Serve on a warmed oval plate, garnished with lemon, parsley and pickled cucumber. Hand dill mayonnaise (see page 91).

Monkfish and Mussel Brochettes

SERVES SIX

900 g (2 lb) monkfish, skinned and boned
18 rashers streaky bacon, rinded and halved
36 mussels, cooked and shelled (see page 98)
50 g (2 oz) butter, melted
60 ml (4 tbsp) chopped fresh parsley
finely grated rind and juice of 1 lime or lemon
4 garlic cloves, skinned and crushed
salt and freshly ground pepper

These brochettes of firm white monkfish and delicate yellow mussels look attractive served on a bed of saffron rice.

1. Cut the monkfish into 42 cubes. Roll up the bacon. Thread the cubed fish, mussels and bacon on to six oiled kebab skewers.

2. Mix together the melted butter, parsley, lime rind and juice, garlic and salt and pepper to taste.

3. Place the brochettes on an oiled grill or barbecue rack. Brush with the butter mixture, then cook under a preheated moderate grill for 15 minutes. Turn the brochettes frequently during cooking and brush with the butter mixture with each turn.

4. Arrange the hot brochettes on a serving platter lined with shredded lettuce. Garnish with bay leaves and lime wedges, if liked.

Monkfish with Lime and Prawns

SERVES FOUR

550 g (1¼ lb) monkfish, skinned
15 ml (1 level tbsp) plain flour
salt and freshly ground pepper
30 ml (2 tbsp) vegetable oil
1 small onion, skinned and chopped
1 garlic clove, skinned and chopped
225 g (8 oz) tomatoes, skinned and chopped
150 ml (¼ pint) dry white wine
finely grated rind and juice of 1 lime
pinch of sugar
100 g (4 oz) peeled prawns
lime slices, to garnish

Green limes, with their tart, acidic flavour, have a high nutritional content; they are an excellent source of citric acid, Vitamins A and C, calcium and phosphorus. To extract the maximum amount of juice from a lime, warm it gently before squeezing.

1. Cut the monkfish into 2.5 cm (1 inch) chunks and toss in the flour seasoned with salt and pepper to taste.

2. Heat the oil in a flameproof casserole, add the onion and garlic and gently fry for 5 minutes. Add the fish and fry until golden.

3. Stir in the tomatoes, wine, lime rind and juice, sugar and salt and pepper. Bring to the boil slowly, stirring occasionally.

4. Cover and cook in the oven at 180°C (350°F) mark 4 for 15 minutes. Add the prawns and continue to cook for a further 15 minutes, until the monkfish is tender. Garnish with lime slices.

Stuffed Plaice Fillets with Mushroom Sauce

SERVES FOUR

4 whole plaice fillets, skinned
225 g (8 oz) cottage cheese with prawns
1.25 ml (¼ tsp) Tabasco sauce, or according to taste
finely grated rind and juice of 1 lemon
salt and freshly ground pepper
225 g (8 oz) button mushrooms, wiped and thinly sliced
90 ml (6 tbsp) dry white wine
5 ml (1 tsp) chopped fresh tarragon or dill or 2.5 ml (½ level tsp) dried
8 unshelled prawns and fresh tarragon or dill sprigs, to garnish

Serve this low calorie dish with jacket-baked potatoes or potatoes boiled in their skins, and a watercress and chicory salad. When selecting the cottage cheese with prawns, choose a good quality brand which is thick and firm textured.

1. Cut each plaice fillet into two lengthways.

2. Drain off any liquid from the cottage cheese, then mash the cheese with half of the Tabasco sauce, the grated lemon rind and salt and pepper to taste.

3. Lay the plaice fillets flat, with their skinned side facing upwards. Divide the cheese filling equally between them, then roll up and secure with cocktail sticks, if necessary.

4. Place the stuffed fish rolls close together in a single layer in a lightly oiled ovenproof dish. Sprinkle the mushrooms around the fish.

Mix the wine with the lemon juice and remaining Tabasco and pour over the fish. Season to taste.

5. Cover the dish with foil and cook in the oven at 180°C (350°F) mark 4 for 20 minutes or until the fish is just tender.

6. Remove the rolls from the liquid and discard the cocktail sticks. Arrange the fish on a warmed serving dish, cover loosely with foil and keep warm in a low oven.

7. Put the cooked mushrooms in a blender or food processor. Add the tarragon or dill and blend until smooth. Pour into a pan and heat through. Taste and adjust seasoning.

8. Pour a little sauce over each plaice roll, then top with a prawn and a tarragon or dill sprig. Serve immediately, with any remaining sauce handed separately in a jug.

Marinated Fish Kebabs

SERVES FOUR

700 g (1½ lb) monkfish fillets, skinned
60 ml (4 tbsp) sunflower oil
juice of 2 limes or 1 lemon
1 small onion, skinned and roughly chopped
2 garlic cloves, skinned and crushed
2.5 ml (½ tsp) fennel seeds
2.5 ml (½ level tsp) dried thyme
freshly ground pepper
1 green pepper, halved, cored and seeded
16 whole cherry tomatoes
8 bay leaves

These easy-to-prepare kebabs would make an excellent summer barbecue dish. providing an unusual alternative to steaks, chicken or chops. Always oil the barbecue grid well first.

1. Cut the monkfish into 4 cm (1½ inch) chunks. Mix the oil, lime or lemon juice, onion, garlic, fennel, thyme and pepper in a blender or food processor until smooth. Toss the fish in this mixture, cover and marinate for at least 2 hours.

2. Meanwhile, place the green pepper in a saucepan of cold water and bring to the boil. Drain and cut into 12 pieces.

3. Thread the fish, green pepper, tomatoes and bay leaves on to four oiled skewers. Reserve the marinade for basting.

4. Cook the kebabs under a preheated moderate grill for about 10 minutes, basting with the marinade and turning once.

Stuffed Plaice with Lemon Sauce

SERVES FOUR

4 small whole plaice, cleaned
65 g (2½ oz) butter
100 g (4 oz) button mushrooms, wiped and finely chopped
100 g (4 oz) white breadcrumbs
90 ml (6 tbsp) chopped fresh parsley
45 ml (3 tbsp) green peppercorns, crushed
finely grated rind and juice of 2 lemons
1.25 ml (¼ level tsp) mustard powder
salt and freshly ground pepper
1 egg, beaten
150 ml (¼ pint) dry white wine
25 g (1 oz) plain flour
60 ml (4 tbsp) single cream
lemon slices and parsley sprigs, to garnish

The plaice in this recipe is filled with a mouthwatering mushroom stuffing with green peppercorns—unripe black peppercorns pickled in brine. Serve with saffron rice and green beans.

1. With the white skin uppermost, cut down the backbone of each of the four plaice. Carefully make a pocket on each side of the backbone by easing the white flesh from the bone.

2. Make the stuffing. Beat 15 g (½ oz) of the butter until softened, then add the mushrooms, breadcrumbs, parsley, 30 ml (2 tbsp) of the peppercorns, lemon rind, mustard and salt and pepper to taste. Mix well and moisten with the egg and a little of the lemon juice.

3. Spoon the stuffing carefully into the pockets in the fish. Then place the fish in a single layer in a buttered ovenproof dish. Pour the wine around the fish and cover loosely with foil. Cook in the oven at 190°C (375°F) mark 5 for 30 minutes.

4. Remove the fish from the dish and place on a warmed serving dish, reserving cooking juices. Cover and keep warm in the oven turned to its lowest setting.

5. Make the sauce. Melt the remaining butter in a saucepan, add the flour and cook gently, stirring, for 1–2 minutes. Remove from the heat and gradually blend in the fish cooking juices, 150 ml (¼ pint) of water and the remaining lemon juice. Bring to the boil, stirring constantly, then lower the heat and stir in remaining peppercorns and cream.

6. To serve the sauce, taste and adjust the seasoning, then pour into a warmed sauceboat. Garnish the fish and serve.

Gingered Plaice with Vegetables

SERVES SIX

900 g (2 lb) plaice fillets, skinned
225 g (8 oz) leeks, trimmed
900 g (2 lb) cauliflower, trimmed
25 g (1 oz) butter
15 ml (1 tbsp) vegetable oil
1 small onion, skinned and finely chopped
5 ml (1 level tsp) ground ginger
15 ml (1 level tbsp) plain flour
150 ml ($\frac{1}{4}$ pint) ginger wine
150 ml ($\frac{1}{4}$ pint) single cream
salt and freshly ground pepper

Available in Britain all the year round, plaice is one of the most popular flat fish. Dabs and flounders are smaller versions of plaice. The baked plaice rolls in this recipe are cooked on a bed of vegetables and flavoured with ginger.

1. Halve the plaice fillets lengthways. Roll up skin side out and secure with a wooden cocktail stick.

2. Cut the leeks into 2.5 cm (1 inch) lengths. Cut the cauliflower into small florets.

3. Heat the butter and oil in a large frying pan with a tight fitting lid, add the cauliflower, leeks, onion and ground ginger and fry for 1–2 minutes. Add the flour and cook, stirring, for 1–2 minutes. Stir in the ginger wine and 150 ml ($\frac{1}{4}$ pint) water. Bring to the boil.

4. Put the rolled plaice on to the vegetables. Cover tightly. Simmer for about 15 minutes or until the cauliflower and fish are just cooked. Remove the cocktail sticks.

5. Pour over the cream, heat gently without boiling. Add salt and pepper to taste.

Turbot à l'Estragon

SERVES FOUR

1.4 kg (3 lb) turbot, cleaned, with head, fins and tail removed
1.1 litres (2 pints) Court Bouillon (see page 88)
lemon slices and parsley sprigs, to garnish
1 quantity Tarragon Butter Sauce, to serve (see page 89)

This quick and easy turbot dish is served with a butter sauce flavoured with tarragon. There are two varieties of tarragon—Russian and French; liquorice-tasting French tarragon is the best.

1. Split the turbot lengthways down the spine and then cut portions across the bone (tronçons).

2. Heat the court bouillon in a saucepan until simmering then add the fish and poach for about 15 minutes until tender.

3. Serve on a warmed round plate, garnished with lemon slices and parsley. Serve the tarragon butter sauce separately.

Skate with Capers and Black Butter

SERVES FOUR

700–900 g (1$\frac{1}{2}$–2 lb) wing of skate
salt
50 g (2 oz) butter
15 ml (1 tbsp) white wine vinegar
10 ml (2 tsp) capers
10 ml (2 tsp) chopped fresh parsley, to garnish

This traditional French way of serving skate is delightfully easy to prepare. Serve with boiled new potatoes and a tossed green salad.

1. Simmer the skate in a pan of salted water for 10–15 minutes until tender. Drain and keep warm.

2. Heat the butter in a pan until lightly browned. Add the vinegar and capers, cook for a further 2–3 minutes and pour it over the fish. Serve at once, garnished with the parsley.

Stuffed Paupiettes of Sole

SERVES SIX

75 g (3 oz) butter
½ medium onion, skinned and chopped
225 g (8 oz) button mushrooms, wiped and trimmed
75 g (3 oz) fresh white breadcrumbs
finely grated rind of 1 lemon
15 ml (1 tbsp) chopped fresh tarragon leaves
salt and freshly ground pepper
18 lemon sole fillets (two from each side of fish), skinned
300 ml (½ pint) dry white wine
30 ml (2 level tbsp) plain flour
about 90 ml (6 tbsp) double cream, at room temperature
fresh tarragon sprigs, to garnish

Although lemon sole has a fine, delicate flavour it is not actually a sole—lemon sole belongs to the plaice family. Its name is a corruption of *limande*, the French word for dab.

1. To make the stuffing, melt 25 g (1 oz) of the butter in a saucepan, add the onion and fry gently until lightly coloured. Meanwhile, slice half the mushrooms and chop the remainder very finely. Put the chopped mushrooms in a bowl with the breadcrumbs, lemon rind and tarragon.

2. Add the softened onion and salt and pepper to taste; stir well until the mixture clings together.

3. Place a sole fillet, skinned side uppermost, on a board. Put a teaspoonful of stuffing on one end of the fillet. Roll the fish up around it. Secure with a cocktail stick.

4. Stand in an upright position in a well-buttered baking dish. Repeat with remaining sole fillets, placing them side by side.

5. Mix together the wine and 150 ml (¼ pint) water and pour over the fish. Cover loosely with foil and bake in the oven at 190°C (375°F) mark 5 for 15 minutes.

6. Remove the fish from the cooking liquid with a slotted spoon and discard the cocktail sticks. Place the fish in a single layer in a warmed serving dish, cover and keep warm. Strain the liquid into a jug.

7. Melt 25 g (1 oz) butter in a saucepan, sprinkle in the flour and cook for 1–2 minutes, stirring. Remove from the heat, then gradually stir in the strained cooking liquid. Bring to the boil, reduce the heat and simmer gently for 5 minutes, stirring until thick.

8. Meanwhile, melt the remaining butter in a frying pan, add the finely sliced mushrooms and fry gently.

9. Whisk the cream into the sauce. Pour a little sauce over each paupiette; then garnish with sliced mushrooms and tarragon sprigs. Pour any remaining sauce into a warmed sauceboat.

Pan-fried Sole with Marsala

SERVES FOUR

8 sole fillets (two from each side of fish), skinned
plain flour
salt and freshly ground pepper
75 g (3 oz) butter
120 ml (8 tbsp) dry Marsala
120 ml (8 tbsp) double cream
chopped fresh parsley and lemon wedges, to garnish

To taste the exquisite flavour of sole at its best it should be cooked simply, as in this Italian recipe.

1. Dip each sole fillet in the flour seasoned with salt and pepper. Coat both sides of the fish evenly, shaking off any excess.

2. Melt the butter in two large frying pans and fry the fish, all at once, for 2–3 minutes on each side until just cooked.

3. Sprinkle over the Marsala and cream, then add salt and pepper to taste. Shake the pans and let the sauce simmer for 2 minutes.

4. Serve immediately, garnished with chopped parsley and lemon wedges.

Turbot au Safran

SERVES FOUR

900 g (2 lb) turbot fillets
25 g (1 oz) butter
50 g (2 oz) shallot or onion, skinned and finely chopped
150 ml (¼ pint) dry white wine
pinch of powdered saffron
600 ml (1 pint) Fish Velouté (see page 89)
150 ml (¼ pint) double cream
100 g (4 oz) tomatoes, skinned, seeded and diced
salt
cayenne pepper
50 g (2 oz) plain flour
100 g (4 oz) clarified butter
parsley sprigs, to garnish

In this recipe, turbot slices are coated in clarified butter before grilling—to clarify butter, heat the butter gently, without browning, until any water is driven off (it will cease to bubble). Leave to stand to let the sediment settle. Strain the melted butter through muslin to clarify, discarding any sediment.

1. Cut the turbot into slices about 1 cm (½ inch) thick.

2. Melt the butter in a saucepan, add the shallot and gently fry until soft but not coloured. Stir in the wine, bring to the boil and boil rapidly to reduce by half. Remove from the heat and stir in the saffron and fish velouté. Bring back to the boil and gently simmer for 10 minutes. Strain and add the cream and diced tomato. Add salt and cayenne pepper to taste.

3. Sprinkle the turbot with salt and cayenne, dip in the flour and shake to remove excess. Coat with the clarified butter. Cook under a preheated grill for 2–3 minutes each side, making sure that the fish is still moist.

4. Coat a warmed oval platter with the sauce and lay the grilled fish on top. Garnish with the parsley and serve immediately.

Mousseline of Sole with Prawns

SERVES SIX

450 g (1 lb) sole fillets, skinned and chopped
50 g (2 oz) peeled prawns
1 egg white, beaten
1.25 ml (¼ level tsp) salt
1.25 ml (¼ level tsp) ground white pepper
450 ml (¾ pint) double cream
3 egg yolks
75 g (3 oz) unsalted butter, softened
10 ml (2 tsp) lemon juice
5 ml (1 tsp) tomato purée
whole prawns, to garnish

A rich-tasting, special occasion starter to impress your guests. The sole and prawn moulds are baked in the oven, then turned out and served with a rich sauce.

1. Combine the chopped sole with the prawns, egg white and seasoning. Purée the mixture in a blender or food processor with 300 ml (½ pint) of the cream.

2. Oil six 150 ml (¼ pint) ovenproof ramekins and press the mixture well down into the dishes. Cover each dish with a round of foil pleated in the centre. Chill for 3 hours.

3. Place the ramekins in a large roasting tin and half fill with boiling water. Bake in the oven at 150°C (300°F) mark 2 for 30–40 minutes. Stand on a rack to drain. Keep warm.

4. Over a pan of hot water, combine the yolks, a knob of butter and lemon juice. Whisk until thick. Remove from the heat; add remaining butter and tomato purée. Whip the remaining cream and add to the sauce. Return to the heat, without boiling. Turn out the mousseline from the ramekins, pour over the sauce and garnish with the whole prawns. Serve immediately.

Opposite: Mixed Seafood Brochettes (see page 35)

Creamed Seafood Vol-au-Vents

SERVES FOUR

450 g (1 lb) whiting fillets
1 bay leaf
few black peppercorns
few parsley sprigs
1 slice onion
300 ml ($\frac{1}{2}$ pint) milk
25 g (1 oz) butter
25 g (1 oz) plain flour
150 ml ($\frac{1}{4}$ pint) single cream
100 g (4 oz) Gruyère cheese, finely grated
1.25 ml ($\frac{1}{4}$ level tsp) ground mace or grated nutmeg
salt and freshly ground pepper
225 g (8 oz) peeled prawns
16 medium-sized (6.5 cm/2$\frac{1}{2}$ inch) frozen vol-au-vent cases
beaten egg, to glaze

Frozen uncooked vol-au-vent cases are readily obtainable and taste so good that it is hardly worth the trouble of making your own. These special seafood vol-au-vents make an impressive dinner party main course with a green vegetable, such as mange-tout.

1. Put the whiting in a saucepan with the bay leaf, peppercorns, parsley and onion. Pour over the milk, then bring to the boil. Cover tightly, remove from the heat and leave until cold.

2. Remove the fish from the pan and reserve the cooking liquid. Flake the flesh of the fish roughly, discarding the skin and any bones.

3. Melt the butter in a saucepan, add the flour and cook gently, stirring, for 1–2 minutes. Remove from the heat and gradually blend in the strained cooking liquid. Bring to the boil, stirring constantly, then simmer for 3 minutes until thickened and smooth.

4. Add the cream and 75 g (3 oz) of the Gruyère cheese. Stir over a very low heat until the cheese has melted.

5. Add the mace or nutmeg and salt and pepper to taste. Gently fold in the flaked white fish and the prawns.

6. Place the vol-au-vent cases on a dampened baking sheet and brush the rims carefully with beaten egg. Bake in the oven at 220°C (425°F) mark 7 for about 15 minutes, or according to packet instructions.

7. Remove the soft centres from the vol-au-vent cases, spoon in the filling, then replace the crisp tops. Serve immediately, piping hot.

Whiting Korma

SERVES FOUR

150 ml ($\frac{1}{4}$ pint) natural yogurt
5 ml (1 tsp) curry paste
1.25 ml ($\frac{1}{4}$ level tsp) ground coriander
1.25 ml ($\frac{1}{4}$ level tsp) ground ginger
1.25 ml ($\frac{1}{4}$ level tsp) turmeric
salt
450 g (1 lb) whiting fillets

A low calorie curried fish recipe to serve with rice and a salad for a light lunch or supper dish.

1. Combine the yogurt with the curry paste, coriander, ginger, turmeric and salt to taste in a dish.

2. Place the unskinned whiting fillets in the marinade, spreading it evenly over the fish. Leave to marinate for 2–3 hours.

3. Arrange the fish with the marinade in a small ovenproof dish. Cook in the oven at 180°C (350°F) mark 4 for about 20 minutes.

Opposite: Wheeler's Fish Soup (see page 37)

Seafood in Saffron Mayonnaise

SERVES FOUR TO SIX

450 g (1 lb) whiting or haddock fillet
1 bay leaf
1 slice lemon
100 g (4 oz) peeled prawns
100 g (4 oz) cooked shelled mussels
few saffron threads
1 egg yolk
150 ml (¼ pint) vegetable oil
10 ml (2 tsp) white wine vinegar
salt and freshly ground pepper
450 g (1 lb) French beans, topped, tailed and cooked
chopped fresh parsley, to garnish

Coated in home-made mayonnaise flavoured and coloured with saffron, this chilled white fish and shellfish dish makes a perfect starter for six people or a main course for four.

1. Place the fish in a large frying pan, cover with water and add the bay leaf and lemon slice. Bring to the boil, then immediately lower the heat and poach gently for 10–15 minutes until cooked. Strain off the poaching liquid, reserving 60 ml (4 tbsp). Cool the fish for at least 20 minutes.

2. Remove the skin and bones and roughly flake the flesh. Place in a bowl with the prawns and mussels, cover and chill.

3. Meanwhile, put the reserved fish liquor in a small saucepan, add the saffron threads and heat gently. Remove from the heat and leave to infuse until cold and golden yellow.

4. Put the egg yolk in a bowl and beat well. Beat in the oil a drop at a time, then continue adding in a thin, steady stream until the mixture is very thick. Stir in half the vinegar and continue beating in the oil until all is incorporated. Stir in the remaining vinegar.

5. Strain the saffron liquid into the mayonnaise and whisk to the consistency of single cream. Add salt and pepper. Chill.

6. Arrange the French beans on a long serving dish. Pile the fish mixture down the centre of the beans and spoon over the mayonnaise. Serve immediately.

Whiting and Caraway Cheese Soufflé

SERVES FOUR

450 g (1 lb) old floury potatoes
450 g (1 lb) whiting fillets
100 g (4 oz) button mushrooms, wiped and thinly sliced
300 ml (½ pint) milk
1 bay leaf
25 g (1 oz) butter
25 g (1 oz) plain flour
2.5 ml (½ tsp) caraway seeds
100 g (4 oz) mature Cheddar cheese, grated
2 eggs, separated
salt and freshly ground pepper

Hot soufflés are a guaranteed success if a few basic rules are followed: make sure the soufflé dish is the size specified; preheat the oven sufficiently; fold in the egg whites with a metal spoon; don't open the oven door during baking.

1. Scrub the potatoes and boil them until tender. Drain and peel, then mash three-quarters of them. Grate the remaining quarter into a bowl and set aside.

2. Meanwhile, place the whiting, mushrooms, milk and bay leaf in a small saucepan. Cover and poach for 15–20 minutes until tender. Drain, reserving the cooking liquid and mushrooms. Flake the fish, discarding the skin, bones and bay leaf.

3. Make the sauce. Melt the butter in a saucepan, add the flour and cook gently, stirring, for 1–2 minutes. Remove from the heat, add the caraway seeds and gradually blend in the reserved cooking liquid. Bring to the boil, stirring constantly, then simmer for 3 minutes until thickened and smooth.

4. Stir the mashed potato into the sauce with 75 g (3 oz) cheese, the egg yolks, fish and mushrooms. Season well.

5. Stiffly whisk the egg whites. Fold into the fish mixture. Turn into a 1.6 litre (2¾ pint) buttered soufflé dish.

6. Sprinkle over the reserved grated potato and remaining grated cheese. Bake in the oven at 190°C (375°F) mark 5 for about 1 hour or until just set and golden brown. Serve immediately.

Italian Fish Stew

SERVES FOUR

good pinch of saffron strands
about 900 g (2 lb) mixed fish fillet, skinned (eg red mullet, bream, bass, brill, monkfish, plaice or cod)
10–12 whole prawns, cooked
10–12 mussels, in their shells
60 ml (4 tbsp) olive oil
1 large onion, skinned and finely chopped
3 garlic cloves, skinned and crushed
2 slices of drained canned pimiento, sliced
450 g (1 lb) tomatoes, skinned, seeded and chopped
2 canned anchovy fillets, drained
150 ml (¼ pint) dry white wine
2 bay leaves
45 ml (3 tbsp) chopped fresh basil
salt and freshly ground pepper
4 slices of hot toast, to serve

When making an Italian fish stew or soup, make sure you choose a good variety of fish. Try to include red or grey mullet and monkfish, as this does not break up easily during cooking.

1. Prepare the saffron water. Soak the saffron strands in a little boiling water for 30 minutes. Meanwhile, cut the fish into chunky bite-sized pieces, keeping firm and delicate textured fish separate. Shell the prawns. Scrub the mussels, ensuring all are closed.

2. Heat the oil in a large heavy-based saucepan, add the onion, garlic and pimiento and fry gently for 5 minutes until soft.

3. Add the tomatoes and anchovies and stir with a wooden spoon to break them up. Pour in the wine and the water and bring to the boil, then lower the heat and add the bay leaves and half the basil. Simmer uncovered for 20 minutes, stirring occasionally.

4. Add the firm fish to the tomato mixture, then strain in the saffron water and add salt and pepper to taste. Cook for 10 minutes, then add the delicate-textured fish and cook for a further 5 minutes or until tender.

5. Add the prawns and mussels and cook, covered, for 5 minutes or until the mussels open. Remove the bay leaves and discard.

6. To serve, put one slice of toast in each of four individual soup bowls. Spoon over the stew, sprinkle with the remaining basil and serve at once.

Mixed Seafood Brochettes

SERVES FOUR

100 g (4 oz) turbot
100 g (4 oz) salmon
450 g (1 lb) shelled scallops
100 g (4 oz) shelled scampi
100 ml (4 fl oz) Marinade for Fish (see page 88)
1 lemon, quartered, and 4 parsley sprigs, to garnish
1 quantity Tarragon Butter Sauce (see page 89) to serve

This delicious selection of seafood is marinated in an olive oil, lemon and herb marinade, then grilled and served with a tarragon-flavoured sauce. Serve on a bed of white, brown or saffron rice with a colourful mixed salad.

1. Cut the turbot and salmon into pieces equal in size to the scallops and scampi.

2. Skewer the pieces of fish alternately on four metal skewers and place in a shallow dish. Pour the marinade over and leave in a cool place for at least 2 hours, turning frequently.

3. Remove the brochettes from the marinade and drain off excess liquid. Place them under a preheated grill and cook for about 15 minutes, turning the brochettes frequently.

4. Serve on a warmed plate, garnished with lemon quarters and parsley sprigs. Hand the tarragon butter sauce separately.

Special Parsley Fish Pie

SERVES FOUR

450 g (1 lb) whiting fillet
300 ml (½ pint) milk, plus 90 ml (6 tbsp)
1 bay leaf
6 peppercorns
1 medium onion, skinned and sliced
salt
65 g (2½ oz) butter
45 ml (3 level tbsp) plain flour
freshly ground pepper
2 eggs, hard-boiled and chopped
150 ml (¼ pint) single cream
30 ml (2 tbsp) chopped fresh parsley
100 g (4 oz) peeled prawns
900 g (2 lb) potatoes, peeled
1 egg, beaten, to glaze

Enriched with cream, this special version of the popular family dish also contains the added attraction of prawns. Pipe the potatoes for the perfect finishing touch.

1. Place the whiting in a saucepan and pour over the 300 ml (½ pint) milk. Add the bay leaf, peppercorns, onion and a pinch of salt. Bring to the boil and simmer for 10 minutes until just tender.

2. Lift from the pan, flake the flesh and remove the skin and bones. Strain the cooking liquid and reserve.

3. Make the sauce. Melt 40 g (1½ oz) of the butter in a saucepan, add the flour and cook gently, stirring, for 1–2 minutes. Remove from the heat and gradually blend in the reserved cooking liquid. Bring to the boil, stirring constantly, then simmer for 3 minutes until thickened. Add salt and pepper to taste.

4. Add the eggs to the sauce with the cream, fish, parsley and prawns. Check the seasoning, then spoon the mixture into a 1.1 litre (2 pint) pie dish.

5. Meanwhile, boil the potatoes, drain and mash without any liquid. Heat the 90 ml (6 tbsp) of milk and remaining butter and beat into the potatoes with salt and pepper to taste.

6. Spoon the potatoes into a piping bag and pipe across the fish mixture. Alternatively, spoon the potato over the fish and roughen the surface with a fork.

7. Bake in the oven at 200°C (400°F) mark 6 for 10–15 minutes, until the potato is set. Brush the beaten egg over the pie. Return to the oven for a further 15 minutes until golden brown.

Bouillabaisse

SERVES SIX

900 g (2 lb) fillets of mixed white fish, skinned, and shellfish
150 ml (¼ pint) olive oil
2–3 medium onions, skinned and sliced
pared rind of 1 orange, finely shredded
1 stick of celery, chopped
225 g (8 oz) tomatoes, skinned and sliced
2 garlic cloves, skinned and crushed
1 bay leaf
2.5 ml (½ level tsp) dried thyme
few parsley sprigs
salt and freshly ground pepper
pinch of saffron strands

Golden saffron is used in this traditional French fish stew to enhance both colour and flavour. Saffron strands are the dried stigma of the autumn flowering crocus: saffron is the most expensive spice in the world. The fish and shellfish to choose from for Bouillabaisse are red mullet, John Dory, monkfish, turbot, whiting, conger eel, prawns, spiny lobster and crab.

1. Cut the fish into fairly large, thick pieces. Heat the oil in a large, heavy-based saucepan and lightly fry the onions for 5 minutes or until soft.

2. Stir half the orange rind into the onion and add the celery, tomatoes, garlic, herbs,

salt and pepper. Dissolve the saffron in a little hot water.

3. Put the fish in with the vegetables. Add the saffron water and just enough cold water to cover. Bring to the boil and simmer, uncovered, for 8 minutes.

4. Add the shellfish and cook for a further 5–8 minutes. Garnish with whole prawns and remaining orange rind.

Bourride

SERVES FOUR

1 egg yolk
10 garlic cloves, skinned
300 ml (½ pint) olive oil
juice of 1 lemon
salt and freshly ground pepper
900 g (2 lb) firm white fish fillets (eg bass, turbot, whiting, monkfish or halibut), skinned
1.1 litres (2 pints) Fish Stock (see page 88)
1 small onion, skinned and thinly sliced
1 leek, trimmed and thinly sliced
1–2 parsley sprigs
1 bay leaf
thin strip of orange rind
1 small baguette (French bread), sliced, to serve
chopped fresh parsley, to garnish

This Mediterranean mixed fish stew with garlic mayonnaise needs no accompaniment other than toasted French bread to mop up the juices.

1. First make the aïoli. Put the egg yolk and 8 roughly chopped garlic cloves in a mortar and crush with a pestle.

2. Add the oil a drop at a time and work until ingredients emulsify and thicken. Then continue adding the oil in a thin, steady stream, beating vigorously until the mixture is very thick and smooth.

3. Beat in the lemon juice and 5 ml (1 tsp) lukewarm water, then add salt and pepper to taste. Set aside in a cool place.

4. Cut the fish into thick chunks and place in a large saucepan. Pour in the stock, then add the onion, leek, parsley, bay leaf and orange rind, with the remaining garlic cloves, halved, and salt and pepper to taste. Cover and simmer for 15 minutes or until tender.

5. Transfer the fish and vegetables with a slotted spoon to a warmed serving dish. Keep warm.

6. Strain the cooking liquid into a jug and blend a few spoonfuls into the aïoli. Toast the sliced baguette and keep warm.

7. Put the aïoli in a heavy-based pan, then gradually whisk in the remaining cooking liquid. Heat through gently, stirring constantly. Adjust seasoning. Pour over the fish and sprinkle with parsley. Serve at once, with the toast.

Wheeler's Fish Soup

SERVES FOUR

1 small onion, skinned
50 g (2 oz) leek, white part only, trimmed
25 g (1 oz) fennel
25 g (1 oz) celery, trimmed
50 ml (2 fl oz) olive oil
1 garlic clove, skinned and crushed
225 g (8 oz) fish, skinned and boned
75 g (3 oz) shellfish, prepared
25 g (1 oz) tomato purée
75 ml (3 fl oz) dry white wine
1.1 litres (2 pints) Fish Stock (see page 88)
good pinch of powdered saffron
50 g (2 oz) tomato, skinned, seeded and diced

Select from monkfish, sole, turbot, salmon or whiting and from scampi, lobster, crab, prawns or mussels for the fish and shellfish in this dish. If using cooked shellfish, add 5 minutes before the end of the cooking time to prevent them from becoming tough.

1. Cut the onion, leek, fennel and celery into thin julienne strips.

2. Heat the olive oil in a saucepan, add the vegetables and garlic and gently fry without colouring until soft.

3. Cut the fish and shellfish into small pieces and add to the vegetables. Stir gently and cook over a low heat to stiffen the flesh without breaking it up.

4. Mix in the tomato purée, then the wine.

5. Bring to the boil and add the fish stock. Reboil and simmer for 20 minutes, skimming frequently.

6. Add salt and pepper to taste, stir in the saffron and cook for a further 5 minutes.

7. Finally, add the diced tomato and some chopped parsley. Serve very hot.

OILY FISH

*O*ily fish range from inexpensive herring and mackerel to far more costly wild salmon and trout. Low in fat, but high in protein and vitamins such as A and D, oily fish are both nutritious and rich in flavour.

Herring and mackerel are available throughout the year, although herring is considered better in the summer months. Luxury Scotch salmon is in season from 1st February to 15th September. Such commercially sold salmon are always caught in the estuary just as they leave the sea, because once they reach the river again they deteriorate in quality. Farmed salmon, however, are in good supply and are available all year round. Salmon trout, or sea trout, is so called because it spends the major part of its life at sea. It is less expensive than salmon and is a useful substitute in salmon recipes. There are two kinds of freshwater trout: brown and rainbow. Rainbow trout is becoming less expensive and more widely available due to commercial trout farming.

RECIPES

OILY FISH

Trout

Salmon

Tuna

Salmon Trout

Eel

Anchovy

Herring

Mackerel

Pilchard

Sprat

Whitebait

Baked Mackerel with Gooseberry Sauce

SERVES FOUR

4 mackerel, cleaned, with heads and tails removed, about 900 g (2 lb) total weight
butter
350 g (12 oz) fresh gooseberries, topped and tailed
15 ml (1 level tbsp) plain flour
200 ml (7 fl oz) chicken stock
30 ml (2 tbsp) snipped fresh chives
salt and freshly ground pepper
sugar

This recipe illustrates one of the most time-honoured ways of serving mackerel. The sharp taste of the gooseberries provides a good contrast to the oily flesh of the fish.

1. Make three slashes across one side of each mackerel to a depth of about 5 mm (¼ inch). Rub over with a little butter. Place the fish, slashed side uppermost, in an ovenproof dish.

2. Bake in the oven at 190°C (375°F) mark 5 for 25–30 minutes.

3. Meanwhile, put the gooseberries and 45 ml (3 tbsp) water in a saucepan. Cover and simmer for 10–15 minutes or until very soft.

Purée in a blender or food processor, or rub through a nylon sieve.

4. Melt 15 g (½ oz) butter in a pan, add the flour and cook gently, stirring, for 1–2 minutes. Remove from the heat and gradually blend in the stock. Add 15 ml (1 tbsp) snipped chives, the gooseberry purée with salt, pepper and sugar to taste. Stir until the mixture is well blended. Bring to the boil, stirring constantly, then simmer for 2–3 minutes. Serve hot with the mackerel, garnished with the remaining chives.

Fish en Papillote

SERVES FOUR

100 g (4 oz) brown rice, cooked
100 g (4 oz) spring onions, trimmed and chopped
small bunch watercress
100 g (4 oz) dried apricots, soaked overnight, then chopped
salt and freshly ground pepper
50 g (2 oz) butter, softened
30 ml (2 tbsp) lemon juice
4 mackerel, about 275–350 g (10–12 oz) each, cleaned and boned
vegetable oil for deep frying

An interesting way to present mackerel — stuffed, wrapped in greaseproof paper and deep fried. This makes a substantial lunch or supper dish that requires no accompaniment.

1. For the stuffing, stir together in a bowl the rice, onion, watercress and apricots, with salt and pepper to taste. Combine with the butter and lemon juice.

2. Lightly grease four 30.5 cm (12 inch) squares of greaseproof paper. Fill each fish cavity carefully with the stuffing, then place the fish on the greaseproof paper and fold the paper to make four sealed parcels.

3. Heat the oil in a deep-fat fryer to 170°C (335°F) and fry the fish parcels for 7 minutes. Remove with a slotted spoon and drain on absorbent kitchen paper. Serve immediately.

ALTERNATIVE STUFFING

salt and freshly ground pepper
100 g (4 oz) wholewheat, soaked overnight, rinsed and drained
50 g (2 oz) butter
2 sticks celery, chopped
2 eating apples, peeled, cored and chopped
5 ml (1 tsp) garden mint

1. Bring a saucepan of salted water to the boil, add the wholewheat and simmer for about 30 minutes until just tender. Drain.

2. Melt the butter in a saucepan, add the celery and apple and fry gently until golden. Remove from the heat and stir in the wholewheat and mint, with salt and pepper.

3. Cool the stuffing. Fill the fish cavities and continue the recipe as shown, left.

Mackerel Parcels

SERVES FOUR

about 25 g (1 oz) butter
8 mackerel fillets
½ large cucumber, sliced
60 ml (4 tbsp) white wine vinegar
30 ml (2 tbsp) chopped fresh mint
5 ml (1 tsp) sugar
salt and freshly ground pepper
natural yogurt and chopped fresh mint, to serve

A versatile dish that can be served hot or cold. Served simply with a salad, these mackerel parcels make a healthy, slimming, main meal; they are also delicious served with tiny new potatoes cooked in their jackets or with a potato salad.

1. Brush eight squares of foil with a little melted butter. Put a mackerel fillet in the centre of each square, skin side down.

2. Arrange the cucumber on one half of the mackerel fillets, then sprinkle with the vinegar, mint, sugar, and salt and pepper to taste. Dot with the remaining butter.

3. Fold the mackerel fillets over to enclose the cucumber filling, then wrap in the foil. Place the foil parcels in a single layer in an ovenproof dish. Cook in the oven at 200°C (400°F) mark 6 for 30 minutes until the fish is tender.

4. To serve, unwrap the foil parcels and carefully place the mackerel fillets in a circle on a warmed platter. Spoon some yogurt in the centre and sprinkle with mint.

Spiced Barbecued Mackerel

SERVES SIX

6 mackerel, about 175 g (6 oz) each, cleaned, heads removed
45 ml (3 tbsp) vegetable oil
2.5 ml (½ level tsp) chilli powder
2.5 ml (½ level tsp) paprika
½ garlic clove, skinned and crushed
grated rind and juice of 1 large orange
orange wedges, to serve

A delicious way of preparing mackerel which provides a tangy, pleasantly charcoaled dish.

1. Make three deep slashes along one side of each fish. Place in a shallow dish.

2. Mix together the oil, chilli powder, paprika, garlic, grated orange rind and 60 ml (4 tbsp) orange juice. Spoon the spice mixture over the mackerel. Cover lightly and marinate in the refrigerator for 2–3 hours. Turn once during this time.

3. Grill or barbecue for about 7 minutes each side, spooning any excess marinade over the fish as they cook. Serve immediately with wedges of fresh orange.

Orange-stuffed Mackerel

SERVES FOUR

25 g (1 oz) butter
1 medium onion, skinned and chopped
50 g (2 oz) long grain rice, cooked
25 g (1 oz) walnuts, chopped
25 g (1 oz) seedless raisins
3 medium oranges
salt and freshly ground pepper
4 mackerel, about 275 g (10 oz) each, cleaned, heads and tails removed and boned
2 egg yolks
5 ml (1 level tsp) cornflour
30 ml (2 tbsp) white wine
parsley sprigs, to garnish

The richness of fresh mackerel, which some people find too oily, can be offset by a zesty orange stuffing, as in this recipe.

1. Melt the butter in a heavy based frying pan and cook the onion until soft. Stir in cooked rice, walnuts and raisins. Grate in orange rind. Season with salt and pepper.

2. Stuff the fish with orange mixture then wrap in greased foil. Bake in the oven at 180°C (350°F) mark 4 for 25–30 minutes or until the fish is tender.

3. Meanwhile beat the egg yolks and cornflour together and stir in the squeezed juice from the oranges and the wine. Cook gently, stirring, until the sauce thickens. Do not boil.

4. Unwrap the fish, then place on a warm serving dish. Pour the sauce over and garnish with parsley sprigs.

Gravad Lax with Dill Sauce

SERVES FOUR OR SIX TO EIGHT AS A STARTER

15 g (½ oz) white peppercorns, coarsely crushed
100 g (4 oz) coarse salt
150 g (5 oz) granulated sugar
1.8 kg (4 lb) fresh salmon, filleted
25 g (1 oz) chopped fresh dill

The salmon in this traditional Scandinavian dish is marinated for three days and is then ready to eat without cooking. It is usually served with dill sauce, Gravad Lax can also be served in the same way as smoked salmon.

1. Mix the coarsely crushed peppercorns with the salt and sugar.

2. Lay one salmon fillet, skin side down, in a dish and spoon over the peppercorn mixture. Sprinkle over the dill and then place the remaining fillet on top, skin side up.

3. Place a board on top of the fish and put weights on top to compress. Refrigerate. Turn the fish and baste with the juices daily, for 3 days. To serve, remove the weights, lift off the top fillet and scrape off the dill and peppercorns. Slice the salmon thinly, cutting down towards the skin across the width of the fillet.

Dill Sauce

SERVES FOUR OR SIX TO EIGHT AS A STARTER

30 ml (2 tbsp) mild Swedish or German mustard
10 ml (2 level tsp) caster sugar
1 egg yolk
150 ml (¼ pint) vegetable oil
30–45 ml (2–3 tbsp) white wine vinegar
30 ml (2 tbsp) chopped fresh dill or 10 ml (2 tsp) dried dillweed

1. Mix the mustard with the sugar and egg yolk. Gradually whisk in the oil as if making mayonnaise, until the sauce is thick. Add the vinegar and dill and mix well.

2. Keep in a cool place for at least 24 hours to allow the flavours to blend.

Salmon Kedgeree

SERVES SIX

350 g (12 oz) salmon
150 ml (¼ pint) dry white wine
2 small onions, skinned and chopped
1 carrot, peeled and sliced
1 celery stick, trimmed and chopped
15 ml (1 tbsp) lemon juice
6 peppercorns
1 bouquet garni
salt and freshly ground pepper
350 g (12 oz) long grain rice
50 g (2 oz) butter
7.5 ml (1½ level tsp) English mustard powder
3 eggs, hard-boiled and quartered
cayenne pepper, to finish
celery leaves or parsley sprigs, to garnish

Kedgeree, sometimes also called khichri, is a rice dish of Anglo-Indian origin. In the days of the Raj it was very popular for breakfast, made with smoked fish rather than the fresh salmon used here. Original recipes for kedgeree are made with curry powder or curry spices and the rice can be quite hot and spicy, however, the delicate flavour of fresh salmon would be overpowered by pungent spices, so they are not used here.

1. Put the salmon in a saucepan, pour in the wine and enough water to cover the fish. Add half of the chopped onions, the carrot, celery, lemon juice, peppercorns, bouquet garni and 5 ml (1 tsp) salt.

2. Bring slowly to the boil, then remove from the heat. Cover tightly and cool.

3. Cook the rice in a saucepan of boiling salted water for 15–20 minutes until tender.

4. Meanwhile, remove the salmon from the liquid and flake the flesh, discarding skin and any bones. Strain the cooking liquid and reserve.

5. Melt half of the butter in a large frying pan, add the remaining onion and fry gently until soft. Drain the rice thoroughly, then add to the onion with the remaining butter. Toss gently to coat in the butter and stir in the mustard powder.

6. Add the flaked salmon and the hard-boiled eggs and a few spoonfuls of the strained cooking liquid to moisten. Heat through. Shake the pan and toss the ingredients gently so that the salmon and eggs do not break up.

7. Transfer to a warmed serving dish and sprinkle with cayenne to taste. Serve immediately, garnished with celery leaves.

Cold Poached Salmon

MAKES FIFTEEN PORTIONS

1 small salmon, about 1.8 kg (4 lb), with tail and fins trimmed and eyes removed

150 ml (¼ pint) dry white wine

1 onion, sliced

1 bay leaf

salt and freshly ground pepper

300 ml (½ pint) liquid aspic jelly

lemon slices, cucumber slices, black olives, whole prawns and endive, to garnish

Mayonnaise, to serve (see page 91)

Cold poached salmon makes an impressive centrepiece for a special occasion. Pay particular attention to the garnishing and allow yourself a little extra time for those important finishing touches. The result can look spectacular.

1. Place the salmon in a fish kettle. Pour over the wine and enough water just to cover the fish. Add the onion, bay leaf, salt and pepper. Bring slowly to the boil, cover and simmer for 25 minutes.

2. Lift the salmon out of the cooking liquid; cool for 2–3 hours. Ease off the skin and place the fish on a serving platter.

3. As the aspic begins to set, brush some over the fish. Leave to set in a cool place for 1–1½ hours. Coat with several layers of aspic.

4. Garnish with lemon slices and cucumber slices and olives. Brush more aspic on top. Arrange endive, whole prawns and sliced cucumber and lemon on the side of the dish and serve with mayonnaise.

Grilled Salmon

SERVES FOUR

4 salmon cutlets, about 225 g (8 oz) each

salt and freshly ground pepper

100 g (4 oz) clarified butter

lemon slices and parsley sprigs, to garnish

1 quantity Béarnaise Sauce, to serve (see page 89)

The cooking time of this dish varies, depending on the thickness of the salmon. It is very important to avoid overcooking and drying out the fish. To make clarified butter, see page 91.

1. Sprinkle the salmon with salt and pepper. Brush with the clarified butter and place on the grill grid.

2. Cook under a preheated grill for about 5 minutes on one side; then turn, brush with more butter and cook the other side for the same length of time.

3. Remove the bones and serve on a warmed platter, garnished with lemon slices and parsley sprigs. Serve the Béarnaise sauce separately.

Poached Salmon

SERVES FOUR

2.3 litres (4 pints) Vinegar Court Bouillon (see page 88)

1 whole salmon, about 1.4–1.8 kg (3–4 lb), cleaned

lemon, parsley sprigs and cucumber slices, to garnish

600 ml (1 pint) Hollandaise Sauce (see page 90), to serve

Scottish salmon, fished for sport in rivers and caught in large quantities in estuaries, are reputed to be the best in the world. Here, the salmon is simply poached whole and served with Hollandaise sauce.

1. Put the bouillon into a fish kettle or large, deep saucepan and bring to the boil. Place the salmon in the pan, with head removed if preferred. Simmer gently for 5–10 minutes per 450 g (1 lb) until tender.

2. Remove the salmon and drain, reserving onion and carrot from the court bouillon. Skin (see page 97) and remove the backbone if preferred.

3. Serve on a large, warmed platter with the few slices of onion and carrot, garnished with lemon, parsley and cucumber. Serve the Hollandaise sauce separately.

Parchment-baked Salmon

SERVES FOUR

4 pieces non-stick parchment or greaseproof paper about 28.5 cm (11 inches) square
50 ml (2 fl oz) dry white wine
100 g (4 oz) cucumber, thinly sliced
4 salmon steaks, about 150 g (5 oz) each
5 ml (1 tsp) fennel seeds, or 2.5 ml (½ tsp) dried dill seeds
25 g (1 oz) butter
salt and freshly ground pepper
fresh dill, to garnish

For maximum flavour, the parchment used here is first soaked in wine. This very convenient way of baking salmon produces excellent moist results. Serve with boiled new potatoes and a tossed green salad.

1. Crush the pieces of parchment together into a flattish round. Place in a small bowl. Pour over the wine. Leave to soak for 1 hour. Push down into the wine occasionally.

2. Separate and open out the parchment sheets. Arrange a circle of cucumber slices in the centre of each sheet. Place a salmon steak on top. Sprinkle with fennel or dill seeds and top with a small piece of butter. Add salt and pepper to taste. Drizzle any remaining white wine over the salmon.

3. Lift up the opposite sides of the parchment and fold together. Twist and tuck under the two shorter ends.

4. Place the parcels on a baking sheet. Bake in the oven at 200°C (400°F) mark 6 for about 15 minutes. Garnish with fresh dill and serve immediately straight from the parchment.

Salmon in Puff Pastry

SERVES SIX

1 bunch watercress, trimmed
45 ml (3 tbsp) soured cream
finely grated rind of ½ lemon
salt and freshly ground pepper
1.1–1.4 kg (2½–3 lb) salmon or salmon trout, filleted and skinned
1 quantity Puff Pastry (see page 92)
beaten egg, to glaze

To make this dish a little more economical, substitute salmon trout for the salmon. For convenience, frozen puff pastry can be used; you will need two 368 g (13 oz) packets, thawed. Stack one on top of the other to roll out, then proceed according to the recipe.

1. Chop the watercress roughly, then place in a bowl with the soured cream. Add the lemon rind with salt and pepper to taste and stir until well mixed.

2. Place two salmon fillets skinned side down on a board and spoon on the prepared watercress filling. Top with the remaining fillets.

3. Roll out the pastry to a rectangle about 30 × 23 cm (12 × 9 inches).

4. Carefully place the fish on the pastry, leaving a 5 mm (¼ inch) border. Brush the edges of the pastry rectangle with some of the beaten egg.

5. Fold the pastry over the fish to enclose it completely. Seal and trim, then knock up the edges. Lift on to a baking sheet and chill for at least 30 minutes.

6. Use the remaining egg to glaze the pastry. Make two small holes in the pastry to allow the steam to escape. Bake in the oven at 200°C (400°F) mark 6 for about 45 minutes until the pastry is well risen and golden brown.

7. To test, make a small slit through the thickest part of the fish—the flesh should begin to flake. Serve warm.

Salmon Mousse

SERVES EIGHT

350 g (12 oz) salmon steaks
1 medium onion, skinned and sliced
75 g (3 oz) carrots, peeled and sliced
2 bay leaves
10 black peppercorns
salt and freshly ground pepper
150 ml (¼ pint) white wine
22.5 ml (4½ level tsp) powdered gelatine
300 ml (½ pint) milk
25 g (1 oz) butter
30 ml (2 level tbsp) plain flour
75 ml (5 tbsp) Mayonnaise (see page 91)
150 ml (¼ pint) whipping cream
red food colouring (optional)
1 egg white
15 ml (1 tbsp) medium sherry
5 ml (1 tsp) rosemary vinegar
10 cm (4 inch) piece of cucumber
Melba toast, to serve

Tail pieces of salmon are usually sold more cheaply than steaks and are a good buy for dishes such as mousses. As long as you have the same weight of salmon flesh as specified in the recipe, you will not notice any difference.

1. Place the salmon steaks in a small shallow pan. Add half the onion and carrot slices, one bay leaf, five of the peppercorns and a good pinch of salt.

2. Spoon over 75 ml (5 tbsp) of the wine with 75 ml (5 tbsp) water and bring slowly to the boil. Cover and simmer gently for 10–15 minutes.

3. Remove salmon pieces, reserving the cooking liquid. Carefully ease off the skin. Using two forks, roughly flake the fish, being careful to remove any bones. Place the fish in a small bowl and keep on one side. Boil the cooking liquid until reduced by half, strain and reserve.

4. For the mousse, spoon 45 ml (3 tbsp) water into a small basin or cup. Carefully sprinkle 15 ml (3 tsp) of the gelatine over the surface; leave for 10 minutes.

5. Put the milk in a saucepan with the remaining onion, carrots, bay leaf and peppercorns and bring to the boil. Pour into a jug and leave to infuse for 10 minutes.

6. Melt the butter in a saucepan, add the flour and cook gently, stirring, for 1–2 minutes. Remove from the heat and gradually blend in the strained milk. Bring to the boil and simmer for 3 minutes. Add salt and pepper to taste. Pour into a bowl and, while still warm, stir in the soaked gelatine in a steady stream until dissolved.

7. Stir the fish into the cool sauce with the reserved cooking liquid. Spoon half at a time into a blender or food processor and switch on for a few seconds only; the fish should retain a little of its texture. Pour into a large bowl.

8. Stir the mayonnaise gently into the salmon mixture. Lightly whip the cream and fold through the mousse. Adjust the seasoning and add a little red food colouring if necessary.

9. Lastly, whisk the egg white until stiff but not dry and fold lightly through the mousse until no traces of white are visible.

10. Pour the mousse into an oiled 18 cm (7 inch) soufflé dish, smooth the surface, cover and refrigerate for about 2 hours to set.

11. Meanwhile, to make aspic, place 30 ml (2 tbsp) very hot water in a bowl and sprinkle in the remaining gelatine. Stir briskly to dissolve. Stir in the remaining white wine, the sherry, vinegar, 90 ml (6 tbsp) water and salt and pepper. Refrigerate the aspic for about 1 hour until completely set.

12. Turn the mousse out on to a flat platter and gently dab with absorbent kitchen paper to remove any oil.

13. Turn the aspic out on to a sheet of damp greaseproof or non-stick paper and chop roughly.

14. Run a fork down the piece of cucumber to form grooves; slice thinly. Place around the side of the mousse. Garnish the mousse with a cucumber twist and surround with chopped aspic. Serve with Melba toast or fingers of toast and butter.

Opposite: Steamed Mullet with Chilli Sauce (see page 15)
Overleaf: Gravad Lax (see page 44)

Salmon and Parma Rolls

MAKES FORTY

100 g (4 oz) unsalted butter
45 ml (3 tbsp) chopped fresh herbs
10 ml (2 tsp) French mustard
freshly ground pepper
10 slices smoked salmon
two 425 g (15 oz) cans asparagus, drained and trimmed
20 slices Parma ham
lemon wedges, to garnish

Ideal as sophisticated buffet fare, this recipe can easily be halved and served as an impressive dinner party starter for four to six people. Italian dried ham, or *prosciutto*, is world famous and the very best is reputed to come from Parma. It should be pale red in colour, sweet and tender and cut wafer thin.

1. Beat the butter to a spreading consistency with the herbs, mustard and pepper to taste. Cut the salmon slices in half lengthways. Spread a little of the flavoured butter mixture over the salmon slices.

2. Place an asparagus spear at one end. Roll the salmon up around the asparagus to enclose it completely, letting the tip of the asparagus protrude slightly at the end of the roll. Try to make the salmon and Parma rolls an even size for that professional look.

3. Repeat using the ham and remaining asparagus. Place the rolls on a serving platter, arranging them in a circle radiating out from the centre. Garnish with lemon wedges and refrigerate the rolls for at least 1 hour before serving.

Baked Trout with Lemon

SERVES SIX

6 medium rainbow trout, cleaned, with heads on
115 g (4½ oz) butter
90 ml (6 tbsp) lemon juice
90 ml (6 tbsp) chopped fresh parsley
salt and freshly ground pepper
25 g (1 oz) almonds, chopped
grated rind of 1 lemon
100 g (4 oz) fresh breadcrumbs
1 egg, beaten
45 ml (3 level tbsp) plain flour
300 ml (½ pint) Fish Stock (see page 88)
2 egg yolks
90 ml (6 tbsp) double cream
lemon slices and fennel tops, to garnish

The flesh of rainbow trout is pale and cream-coloured when cooked and the texture soft and smooth. The creamy sauce here enhances the delicate flavour of the trout.

1. Make three or four diagonal slashes about 5 mm (¼ inch) deep on either side of each trout. Place the fish, side by side, in a shallow, ovenproof dish.

2. Melt 75 g (3 oz) of the butter in a small saucepan. Leave to cool, then mix in the lemon juice, 75 ml (5 tbsp) of the parsley and salt and pepper to taste. Pour over the fish. Cover with cling film and leave in a cool place (not the refrigerator) for 2 hours, turning and basting once.

3. Meanwhile, make the stuffing. Mix together the almonds, lemon rind, breadcrumbs, seasoning, remaining parsley and egg to bind.

4. Remove the cling film from the dish and fill the cavities of each fish with the stuffing.

Cover the dish with foil and bake in the oven at 180°C (350°F) mark 4 for about 40 minutes until tender.

5. While the fish is cooking, make the sauce. Melt the remaining butter in a small saucepan, add the flour and cook gently, stirring, for 1–2 minutes. Remove from the heat and gradually blend in the stock. Bring to the boil, stirring constantly, then simmer for 3 minutes until thickened and smooth.

6. Remove from the heat. Blend the egg yolks with the cream and stir into the sauce. Add salt and pepper to taste. Remove the foil from the fish and stir the cooking juices into the sauce. Reheat gently, stirring continuously, without boiling the sauce.

7. Pour some of the sauce beside the fish, garnish with lemon slices and fennel tops and serve the remaining sauce separately.

Overleaf: Salmon Kedgeree (see page 45)
Opposite: Swedish Herrings (see page 54)

Tarragon-stuffed Trout

SERVES SIX

100 g (4 oz) peeled prawns
50 g (2 oz) butter
1 medium onion, skinned and finely chopped
225 g (8 oz) button mushrooms, wiped and roughly chopped
5 ml (1 tsp) chopped fresh tarragon or 1.25 ml (¼ level tsp) dried
salt and freshly ground pepper
25 g (1 oz) long grain rice, cooked
30 ml (2 tbsp) lemon juice
6 rainbow trout, about 225 g (8 oz) each, cleaned, with heads on
tarragon sprigs, to garnish

Rainbow trout is easily recognised by its attractive silver skin and the shimmer of pink running down the centre of the fish from head to tail. It is a freshwater fish, now reared in large quantities on trout farms, and therefore available all year round.

1. Make the stuffing. Cut up each of the peeled prawns into two or three pieces.

2. Melt the butter in a large frying pan, add the finely chopped onion and fry for 5 minutes until golden brown.

3. Add the mushrooms with the tarragon and salt and pepper to taste. Cook over high heat for 5–10 minutes until all excess moisture has evaporated. Leave to cool for about 30 minutes.

4. Carefully mix the prawns, rice, lemon juice and mushroom mixture together and adjust the seasoning.

5. Place the fish side by side in a lightly buttered ovenproof dish and stuff each with the mixture. Cover and cook in the oven at 180°C (350°F) mark 4 for about 30 minutes or until cooked.

6. To serve, garnish with tarragon. Accompany with boiled new potatoes and mange tout or petits pois.

Trout Poached in Wine

SERVES FOUR

4 small trout, cleaned, with heads on
salt and freshly ground pepper
50 g (2 oz) butter
1 large onion, skinned and sliced
2 celery sticks, trimmed and sliced
2 carrots, peeled and very thinly sliced
300 ml (½ pint) dry white wine
bouquet garni
15 ml (1 level tbsp) plain flour
lemon wedges and chopped fresh parsley, to garnish

For this recipe you will need freshwater trout—river, rainbow or lake trout—which are now becoming increasingly available. Look for shiny, slippery skin and bright eyes—both indications of freshness.

1. Sprinkle the insides of each trout with salt and pepper to taste.

2. Melt 25 g (1 oz) of the butter in a small saucepan, add the onion, celery and carrots and stir well to cover with butter. Cover and sweat for 5 minutes.

3. Lay the vegetables in a greased casserole and arrange the fish on top. Pour over the wine and add the bouquet garni.

4. Cover tightly and cook in the oven at 180°C (350°F) mark 4 for about 25 minutes until the trout are cooked.

5. Transfer the trout and vegetables to a warmed serving dish and keep hot, reserving the cooking juices and discarding the bouquet garni.

6. Blend together the remaining butter and the flour. Whisk in pieces into the sauce and simmer gently, stirring, until thickened. Pour into a sauceboat or jug to serve separately. Garnish the trout with lemon wedges and parsley.

Italian Marinated Trout

SERVES FOUR

4 whole trout, about 225 g (8 oz) each, cleaned, with heads on
30 ml (2 level tbsp) plain flour
30 ml (2 tbsp) olive oil
1 small bulb Florence fennel, trimmed and finely sliced
1 medium onion, skinned and finely sliced
300 ml (½ pint) dry white Italian wine
finely grated rind and juice of 1 orange
salt and freshly ground pepper
orange slices and chopped fennel tops, to garnish

As the trout needs to be marinated for at least 8 hours, it is ideal for the busy cook who can fit in the preparation at a convenient time in advance. Serve as a cold summer supper dish with hot garlic or herb bread and a mixed salad.

1. Dip the trout in the flour. Heat the oil in a frying pan and fry the fish gently for 4 minutes on each side. Using a fish slice, transfer the fish to a shallow dish.

2. With a sharp knife, score the skin diagonally, being careful not to cut too deeply into the flesh. Set the trout aside while preparing the marinade.

3. Add the fennel and onion to the frying pan and fry for 5 minutes. Add the wine, orange rind and juice and salt and pepper to taste. Bring to the boil. Boil rapidly for 1 minute, add the chopped fennel tops and pour immediately over the fish. Leave the trout to cool completely in the marinade.

4. Marinate in the refrigerator for at least 8 hours, but no more than three days.

5. Serve at room temperature, garnished with orange slices.

Poached Salmon Trout

SERVES SIXTEEN SMALL BUFFET PORTIONS

1–2 salmon trout, total weight cleaned and prepared (see page 96) about 1.8 kg (4 lb)
150 ml (¼ pint) medium dry white wine
1 small onion, skinned and sliced
1 bay leaf
salt and freshly ground pepper
300 ml (½ pint) liquid aspic jelly with 45 ml (3 tbsp) sherry added
slices of lemon, cucumber and endive, to garnish
Mayonnaise, to serve (see page 91)

Salmon trout are the larger of the species and are called sea trout because they have migrated from the rivers to the sea. These trout are named after salmon because their flesh is salmon pink and firm, and can be used as a cheaper alternative to fresh salmon. Serve this dish as a cold buffet centrepiece.

1. Place the trout in a fish kettle or a deep roasting container. Pour over the wine with sufficient water just to cover the fish. Add the onion and bay leaf with salt and pepper to taste.

2. Bring slowly to the boil, cover and simmer very gently for about 25 minutes, or until the fish begins to come away from the bone. Lift out of the liquid, then cool. Ease off the skin. Place the fish on a serving platter.

3. As the aspic begins to set, brush some over the fish. Leave to set. Coat with several layers of aspic in the same way. Warm the aspic gently if necessary.

4. Garnish the fish with lemon and cucumber. Brush more aspic on top of the garnish. Arrange endive on the side of the dish and serve with mayonnaise.

Lentil Tuna Savoury

SERVES FOUR

175 g (6 oz) red lentils
15 g (½ oz) butter
1 small onion, skinned and finely chopped
175 g (6 oz) tuna steak, cooked, or 184 g (6½ oz) can tuna
1 large egg
salt and freshly ground pepper
150 ml (¼ pint) milk
25 g (1 oz) salted peanuts, finely chopped

This nutritious dish could easily be adapted to make a healthy slimmer's meal by substituting low-calorie spread for the butter and skimmed milk instead of whole milk. Serve with a green vegetable or salad.

1. Place the lentils in a saucepan with 600 ml (1 pint) water. Bring to the boil, then simmer for 20–25 minutes until the lentils are just tender and most of the liquid has evaporated. Stir occasionally.

2. Melt the butter in a saucepan and gently fry the onion without colouring until softened.

3. Meanwhile, roughly flake the tuna. Remove the pan of onion from the heat and stir in the tuna.

4. Beat the lentils, egg and milk into the tuna mixture. Add salt and pepper to taste. Spoon into a shallow 1.1 litre (2 pint) ovenproof dish. Sprinkle the peanuts over the dish. Bake in the oven at 180°C (350°F) mark 4 for 25–30 minutes.

Tuna and Cheese Soufflé Flan

SERVES FOUR

225 g (8 oz) plain flour
30 ml (2 tbsp) grated Parmesan cheese
150 g (5 oz) butter
2 eggs, separated
175 g (6 oz) tuna steak, cooked
200 ml (7 fl oz) milk
5 ml (1 tsp) lemon juice
100 g (4 oz) smoked Austrian cheese, grated
salt and freshly ground pepper

Tuna, also called tunny, is a powerful torpedo-shaped fish found in all tropical and temperate seas. To cook it for this recipe, simply grill or braise in the oven until tender. If it is difficult to obtain fresh tuna, use a 184 g (6½ oz) can.

1. Mix 175 g (6 oz) of the flour with the Parmesan in a bowl. Rub in 75 g (3 oz) of the butter until the mixture resembles breadcrumbs. Bind to a manageable dough with 1 egg yolk and a little water. Chill for 10 minutes.

2. Roll out the dough and use to line a 20.5 cm (8 inch) plain flan ring placed on a baking sheet. Chill again for 10–15 minutes then bake blind in the oven at 200°C (400°F) mark 6 for 10–15 minutes until set but not browned.

3. Lightly break up the tuna. Melt the remaining butter in a saucepan, add the remaining flour and cook gently, stirring, for 1–2 minutes. Remove from the heat and gradually blend in the milk and lemon juice. Bring to the boil, stirring constantly, then simmer for 3 minutes. Gently stir in the tuna, 75 g (3 oz) of the cheese and the remaining egg yolk. Add a little salt and pepper to taste.

4. Stiffly whisk the egg whites and fold into the tuna mixture. Spoon into the prepared pastry case. Sprinkle over the remaining cheese and return to the oven for 35–40 minutes until risen and golden. Serve immediately.

Grilled Herrings with Horseradish

SERVES FOUR

4 herrings, about 200 g (7 oz) each, cleaned and boned
50 g (2 oz) walnut pieces, finely chopped
30 ml (2 tbsp) creamed horseradish
15 ml (1 tbsp) medium oatmeal
150 ml (¼ pint) single cream
5 ml (1 tsp) lemon juice
vegetable oil for grilling

The pungent root horseradish is a member of the mustard family. Creamed horseradish is milder than horseradish relish and, therefore, well suited as a flavouring for these herrings, mixed with cream and walnut pieces.

1. Make 2–3 diagonal shallow cuts in the flesh on both sides of the herrings.

2. Mix together the walnut pieces, horseradish, oatmeal, cream, lemon juice and salt and pepper to taste.

3. Put the fish in a foil-lined grill pan and brush lightly with oil. Cook under a preheated grill for about 5 minutes on each side. Spread the horseradish mixture over the top of each herring. Grill for a further 3–4 minutes until the herrings are cooked and golden brown.

Soft Roes with Grapes

SERVES TWO

225 g (8 oz) soft herring roes
15 ml (1 level tbsp) plain flour
25 g (1 oz) butter
100 g (4 oz) seedless white grapes, halved
60 ml (4 tbsp) soured cream
15 ml (1 tbsp) lemon juice
15 ml (1 tbsp) chopped fresh parsley
salt and freshly ground pepper
2 large slices wholemeal toast

Both hard and soft roes can be bought fresh from the fishmongers; they are also available canned. Soft roes on toast are often served as a popular snack or family tea. Here they are enriched with soured cream with halved grapes adding an original touch.

1. Drain the roes, remove any black threads, then dry on absorbent kitchen paper. Cut them into fork-sized pieces.

2. Mix the roes and flour together. Melt the butter in a small frying pan, add the roes and fry for 2–3 minutes, stirring occasionally. Stir in the grapes and fry, stirring, for another minute.

3. Blend in the soured cream, lemon juice, parsley and salt and pepper to taste. Bring to the boil, simmer for 1 minute. Taste and adjust the seasoning again.

4. Spoon the roe and grape mixture on to the slices of toast to serve.

Deep-fried Whitebait

SERVES FOUR

700 g (1½ lb) whitebait
about 300 ml (½ pint) milk
plain flour, to coat
salt
cayenne pepper
vegetable oil, for deep frying
1 lemon, quartered, and 4 parsley sprigs, to garnish

Silvery whitebait are between 2.5–7.5 cm (1–3 inches) long and are the small fry of various oily fish, mainly herring and sprat. They are eaten whole and are most popular as a deep fried starter.

1. Dip the whitebait in the milk. Drain and then roll in the flour, seasoned with salt and cayenne, to coat them evenly. Shake the fish gently in a sieve to remove excess flour and to keep them separate.

2. Heat the oil in a deep-fat fryer to 180°C (350°F), add the fish in batches and fry for about 1–2 minutes per batch until golden brown and crispy.

3. Remove from the pan, drain off excess oil and place on absorbent kitchen paper. Sprinkle with salt and cayenne pepper to taste and serve immediately on a warmed platter, garnished with lemon quarters and parsley sprigs.

Swedish Herrings

SERVES FOUR

8 herring fillets
salt and freshly ground pepper
4 whole cloves
2 dried chillies
12 peppercorns
1 bay leaf
1 blade of mace
60 ml (4 tbsp) malt vinegar
75 ml (5 tbsp) tarragon vinegar
1 shallot, skinned and finely chopped
lemon slices, to garnish
150 ml (¼ pint) soured cream, to serve

This traditional Scandinavian dish would make an excellent summer lunch dish, served with warm crusty bread and salad. Alternatively, halve the quantities stated and serve as a tempting starter.

1. Sprinkle the herring fillets with salt and freshly ground pepper to taste, then roll up from the head end, skin side outermost.

2. Arrange in a casserole and add the cloves, chillies, peppercorns, bay leaf and mace. Cover with the vinegars and 150 ml (¼ pint) water. Sprinkle the shallot on top.

3. Cover and cook in the oven at 170°C (325°F) mark 3 for about 45 minutes or until the herring fillets are tender.

4. Transfer the fish carefully to a serving dish and strain or pour the liquor over. Leave to cool for about 2–3 hours.

5. Garnish with lemon slices and serve cold with soured cream.

Wine-braised Eel

SERVES SIX

900 g (2 lb) eel, or 1.4 kg (3 lb) mackerel, cleaned
50 g (2 oz) butter
30 ml (2 tbsp) vegetable oil
1 large onion, skinned and roughly chopped
350 g (12 oz) celery, trimmed and roughly chopped
450 g (1 lb) peppers, green red and yellow, cored, seeded and roughly chopped
1 garlic clove, skinned and crushed
5 ml (1 level tsp) dried basil
15 ml (1 level tbsp) plain flour
300 ml (½ pint) dry white wine
grated rind of 1 lemon
salt and freshly ground pepper
30 ml (2 tbsp) chopped fresh parsley, to garnish

Eels are available all year round. They are rich and nourishing, and should be used as soon as possible after buying. Here they are cooked until tender in the oven with white wine and vegetables.

1. To skin the eel, hold it in a cloth to prevent it slipping, then cut through the skin round the neck and right down the length of the body. Using another cloth to get a good grip, pull back the skin firmly to peel off from neck to tail.

2. Chop the eel into 5 cm (2 inch) pieces. If using mackerel, chop similarly.

3. Heat the butter and oil in a shallow flameproof casserole, add the onion, celery, peppers, garlic and basil and fry gently for 3–4 minutes until softened.

4. Mix in the flour. Cook, stirring, for 1–2 minutes, then add the wine and lemon rind. Bring to the boil, then remove from heat.

5. Place the fish pieces on top of the vegetable mixture and add salt and pepper to taste. Cover tightly. Cook in the oven at 180°C (350°F) mark 4 for 25–30 minutes. Adjust the seasoning and garnish with chopped parsley.

Sardines with Herbs

SERVES FOUR TO SIX

60 ml (4 tbsp) chopped fresh mint
60 ml (4 tbsp) chopped fresh parsley
60 ml (4 tbsp) chopped fresh sage
grated rind of 2 lemons
120 ml (8 tbsp) lemon juice
300 ml ($\frac{1}{2}$ pint) vegetable oil
1 large onion, skinned and finely sliced
salt and freshly ground pepper
900 g (2 lb) sardines (at least 12)
lemon wedges, to garnish

Sardines are small oily fish belonging to the herring family. They have a high fat content which prevents them being transported long distances; hence they are more widely available canned. Fresh sardines make a perfect starter or delicious snack.

1. Reserving 15 ml (1 tbsp) of each herb, mix together the remainder with the lemon rind, juice, oil, onion and salt and pepper to taste.

2. Put the sardines under a preheated grill and cook for 5–7 minutes each side, basting with the herb dressing.

3. Arrange on a shallow dish, cover with the herb dressing and leave to cool.

4. Sprinkle with the reserved herbs before serving and garnish with lemon wedges.

Pasta and Anchovy Salad with Garlic Dressing

SERVES SIX

two 50 g (2 oz) cans anchovies in oil
45 ml (3 tbsp) milk
350 g (12 oz) small pasta shapes
salt and freshly ground pepper
1 garlic clove, skinned and roughly chopped
75 ml (3 fl oz) vegetable oil
juice of $\frac{1}{2}$ lemon
185 g (6$\frac{1}{2}$ oz) can pimientos, drained
60 ml (4 tbsp) Mayonnaise (see page 91)

Don't use the tiniest pasta shapes, which are normally only for soups, for this dish. Shapes like shells, spirals and bows, which can hold salad dressings, are best.

1. Drain the anchovies, place in a bowl and add the milk. Leave to soak for 30 minutes to remove excess salt.

2. Meanwhile, bring a large saucepan of salted water to the boil, add the pasta and cook according to the packet instructions until *al dente*.

3. Drain the anchovies again and rinse under cold running water. Pat dry with absorbent kitchen paper.

4. Reserve a few of the anchovies whole for garnishing and pound the remainder to a paste with the garlic. Add the oil and lemon juice gradually, whisking with a fork until thick. Add pepper to taste.

5. Drain the pasta and turn into a large bowl. Pour in the dressing immediately and toss well to mix. Leave to cool, then cover and chill for at least 2 hours, or overnight if more convenient.

6. Cut the pimientos into thin strips. Add to the pasta salad, reserving a few for garnish. Add the mayonnaise and toss gently to mix. Taste and adjust seasoning.

7. Pile the salad into a serving bowl and arrange the remaining whole anchovies and pimiento strips in a lattice pattern over the top. Serve at room temperature.

SHELLFISH

Shellfish are divided into two groups—crustaceans and molluscs. Crustaceans include prawns, crabs, lobsters, shrimps and scampi, and have firm, sweet flesh with fairly hard-jointed shells. Molluscs include oysters, mussels, clams, scallops, cockles, winkles and whelks and their flesh is usually protected by a hard shell. Cephalopods, such as squid, have also been included in this section. They have bag-like bodies, and tentacles, but have no true skeleton.

Shellfish should be eaten absolutely fresh; indeed, mussels and clams are always sold live. Mussels, oysters, clams, cockles and scallops are at their best during the colder months, whereas crabs and lobsters are best in the summer.

RECIPES

SHELLFISH & CRUSTACEA

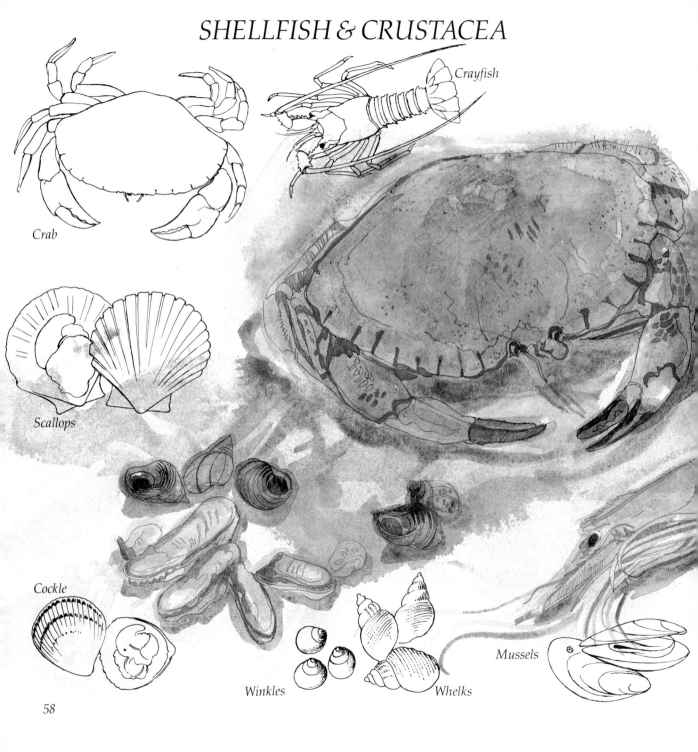

Crab

Crayfish

Scallops

Cockle

Winkles

Whelks

Mussels

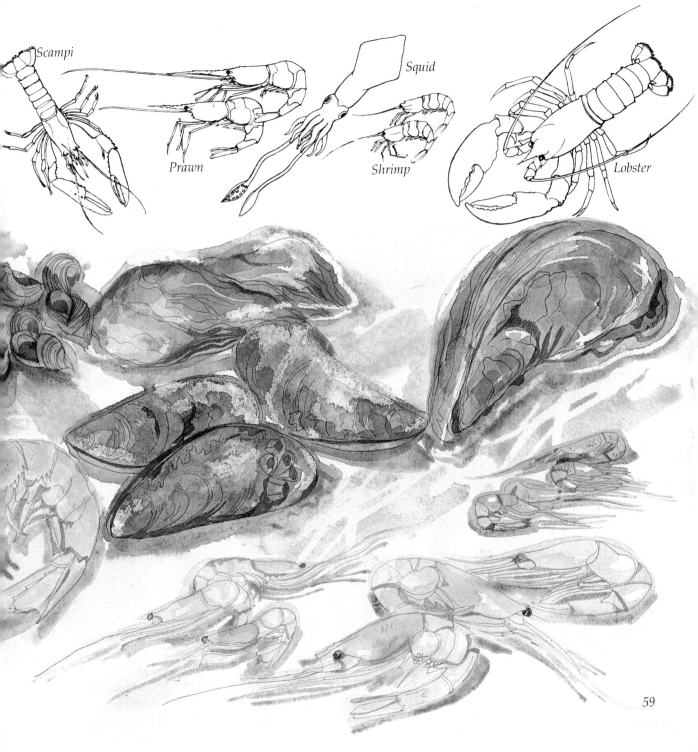

Scampi

Prawn

Squid

Shrimp

Lobster

59

Fettuccine with Clam Sauce

SERVES FOUR

about 2.3 litres (4 pints) clams, cleaned
15 ml (1 tbsp) olive oil
1 onion, skinned and finely chopped
2–3 garlic cloves, skinned and crushed
700 g (1½ lb) tomatoes, skinned and roughly chopped, or one 397 g (14 oz) can tomatoes
30 ml (2 tbsp) chopped fresh parsley
salt and freshly ground pepper
400 g (14 oz) fettuccine or other long thin pasta

Obtainable in certain areas all year round, clams are at their best in the autumn. This pasta dish is ideal as a lunch or supper.

1. Put the clams in a large saucepan with 300 ml (½ pint) water, cover and bring to the boil. Cook over high heat until all the shells are open (about 10 minutes), shaking the pan occasionally. If some remain closed after this time, discard them. Strain the clams, discarding the cooking liquid. Remove the meat from the shells (reserving a few whole ones to garnish, if liked).

2. Heat the olive oil in a saucepan, add the onion and garlic and fry gently for 5 minutes until soft but not coloured. Stir in the tomatoes and their juice, bring to the boil and cook for 15–20 minutes until slightly reduced.

3. Stir the drained clams into the sauce with 15 ml (1 tbsp) parsley and salt and pepper to taste. Remove from the heat.

4. Cook the fettuccine in a large pan of boiling salted water for 8–10 minutes until just tender.

5. Reheat the sauce just before the pasta is cooked and taste and adjust seasoning. Drain the fettuccine well, tip into a warmed serving dish. Season with pepper and pour over the hot clam sauce. Sprinkle with the remaining parsley to garnish.

Cockle and Leek Pies

SERVES FOUR

grated rind and juice of 1 lemon
350 g (12 oz) shelled cooked cockles—about 600 ml (1 pint), well rinsed
25 g (1 oz) butter
350 g (12 oz) leeks, trimmed and thickly sliced
30 ml (2 level tbsp) plain flour
150 ml (¼ pint) milk
198 g (7 oz) can sweetcorn kernels, drained
pinch of grated nutmeg
freshly ground pepper
100 g (4 oz) Puff Pastry (see page 92)

If using fresh cockles in their shells, first prepare as on page 98. To cook, put in a large pan with a little water. Heat gently, shaking the pan, for about 5 minutes or until the shells have opened. Drain well, remove the cockles and use as described below.

1. Stir the grated rind and 30 ml (2 tbsp) lemon juice into the cockles.

2. Heat the butter in a medium saucepan, add the leeks and fry gently for 1–2 minutes. Sprinkle over the flour. Cook, stirring, for 1–2 minutes before adding the milk, sweetcorn and nutmeg. Add pepper to taste. Allow to cool.

3. Stir in the cockles and juices. Divide the mixture between four 150 ml (¼ pint) ovenproof plates or scallop shells.

4. Roll out the pastry, divide into four and use to cover the fillings. Pressing down at the edges, trim the pastry, leaving an extra 5 mm (¼ inch) all round. Pull the back of a knife through the pastry at regular intervals to create a scalloped edge.

5. Bake in the oven at 200°C (400°F) mark 6 for about 30 minutes or until well risen and golden. Serve immediately.

Avocado with Crab

SERVES FOUR

30 ml (2 tbsp) vegetable oil
1 small onion, skinned and very finely chopped
10 ml (2 tsp) garam masala
150 ml (¼ pint) thick Mayonnaise (see page 91)
10 ml (2 tsp) tomato purée
finely grated rind and juice of ½ lemon
salt and freshly ground pepper
225 g (8 oz) white crab meat, flaked
2 ripe avocados
lemon twists and paprika, to garnish

This luxury dinner party starter with its rich blend of flavours, is nevertheless quick and easy to prepare. If made in advance, brush the avocado flesh with a little lemon juice to prevent discolouring.

1. Heat the oil in a small saucepan, add the onion and garam masala and fry gently, stirring constantly, for 5 minutes until the onion is soft. Turn into a bowl and cool.

2. Add the mayonnaise to the cold onion with the tomato purée, lemon rind and juice. Add salt and pepper to taste.

3. Fold the crab meat gently into the mayonnaise, taking care not to break up the pieces of crab.

4. Cut the avocados in half lengthways and then prise the halves apart by twisting them in opposite directions. Remove the stones from the avocados by gently easing them out with the fingers.

5. Place an avocado half on each serving dish, then pile the filling into each half. Garnish with lemon twists and a sprinkling of paprika, and serve immediately.

Hot Crab and Ricotta Quiches

SERVES SIX

175 g (6 oz) Shortcrust Pastry (see page 93)
2 eggs
150 ml (¼ pint) single cream
150 ml (¼ pint) milk
225 g (8 oz) crab meat, flaked
175 g (6 oz) Ricotta cheese, crumbled
30 ml (2 tbsp) grated Parmesan
salt and freshly ground pepper

These versatile individual quiches make perfect hot buffet fare, or can be served as a substantial starter or lunch dish. If preferred, one large quiche can be made instead. Accompany with a green salad.

1. Roll out the pastry and use to line six 8.5 cm (3½ inch) fluted, loose-bottomed, flan tins or a 20.5 cm (8 inch) flan dish placed on a baking sheet. Bake blind in the oven at 200°C (400°F) mark 6 for 10–15 minutes.

2. Meanwhile, whisk the eggs, cream and milk together in a bowl. Add the crab meat and Ricotta to the egg mixture with the Parmesan and plenty of salt and pepper.

3. Pour into the flan cases.

4. Reduce the oven temperature to 190°C (375°F) mark 5 and bake the quiches for 35 minutes until golden.

Lobster Thermidor

SERVES FOUR

4 lobsters, about 450–550 g (1–1¼ lb) each, cooked and shelled lengthways, reserving shells

25 g (1 oz) butter

1 shallot, skinned and finely chopped

150 ml (¼ pint) dry white wine

5 ml (1 tsp) English mustard

7.5 ml (½ tbsp) chopped fresh parsley

1 quantity Mornay Sauce (see page 90)

50 ml (2 fl oz) Hollandaise Sauce (see page 90)

50 ml (2 fl oz) double cream

Reserve this classic, and probably most famous, lobster dish for very special occasions. It is important not to cook the lobster meat further when heating it in the white wine mixture as it may toughen.

1. Cut the lobster meat into thick slices and remove the claw meat from the bones.

2. Melt the butter in a frying pan, add the shallot and cook gently without colouring. Pour in the white wine and boil to reduce the volume by half.

3. Dilute the mustard with a little water and add to the pan with the chopped parsley.

4. Reduce the heat to very low and carefully stir in the lobster. Heat through gently without cooking the lobster further.

5. Gently heat the mornay sauce, then spoon a little into the reserved lobster shells. Arrange the pieces of lobster over the sauce in each shell.

6. Add the hollandaise sauce and cream to the remaining mornay sauce and coat the lobster.

7. Brown under a preheated grill until golden. Serve immediately on a warmed oval plate.

Cream of Lobster Soup

SERVES FOUR

450 g (1 lb) lobster shells

50 g (2 oz) butter

1 small onion, skinned and chopped

1 small carrot, peeled and chopped

30 ml (2 tbsp) brandy

15 ml (1 tbsp) tomato purée

150 ml (¼ pint) dry white wine

1.1 litres (2 pints) Fish Stock (see page 88)

1 bouquet garni

50 g (2 oz) rice flour

salt and cayenne pepper

150 ml (¼ pint) double cream

150 g (5 oz) fresh, frozen or canned lobster meat, if liked

It was for the famous Thursday Club that the first Wheeler's lobster soup laced with brandy was exclusively prepared. The shell plays an important part in the taste.

1. Break the shells into large pieces.

2. Melt the butter in a saucepan, add the shells, onion and carrot, and cook gently without colouring for a few minutes, stirring frequently.

3. In a small saucepan, warm the brandy, and ignite. Let the flames die down, and pour over the vegetables. Mix in the tomato purée and add the white wine, stock, and bouquet garni. Bring to the boil, turn down the heat and simmer for 15–20 minutes.

4. Dilute the rice flour with a little cold water, add to the soup and bring back to the boil to thicken it.

5. Remove the shells, crush them and return to the soup. Cook for a further 20 minutes.

6. Strain the soup through muslin or a sieve, then return to the pan and bring to the boil. Add cayenne and salt, to taste. Stir in the cream and lobster flesh, if liked. Heat gently and serve.

Ragoût of Lobster

SERVES FOUR

25 g (1 oz) butter
1 shallot, skinned and finely chopped
15 g (½ oz) fresh root ginger, peeled and finely chopped
4 spring onions, trimmed and cut into thin rings
75 ml (3 fl oz) dry white wine
1 quantity Fish Velouté (see page 89)
4 lobsters, about 450–550 g (1–1¼ lb) each, cooked and shelled
salt and freshly ground pepper
100 ml (4 fl oz) double cream

Lobster is bluish-black in its natural state, but turns a dramatic cardinal red when cooked. Serve this rich and creamy lobster main course simply with plain boiled rice.

1. Melt the butter in a frying pan, add the shallot and cook gently without colouring. Stir in the ginger, spring onion and wine. Boil rapidly to reduce by half, then add the velouté and reboil.

2. Add the pieces of lobster, reheating gently without further cooking. Add salt and pepper to taste and stir in the cream.

Grilled Lobster

SERVES FOUR

Vinegar Court Bouillon, to cover lobsters (see page 88)
4 lobsters, about 450–550 g (1–1¼ lb) each
50 g (2 oz) butter, melted
lemon slices and parsley sprigs, to garnish
1 quantity Béarnaise Sauce (see page 89) or beurre fondu, to serve

To make beurre fondu, simply melt the butter gently in a pan. Sprinkle with salt and freshly ground pepper and a few drops of lemon juice.

1. Place the court bouillon in a large saucepan, add the lobsters and bring to the boil. Simmer for 15 minutes to three-quarters cook the lobsters. This prevents the lobster flesh drying out under the grill.

2. Split the lobster in half lengthways, remove the sac from the head and tail from the body (see page 100).

3. Sprinkle with salt and pepper to taste and brush with the melted butter. Cook under a preheated moderate grill for about 10 minutes.

4. Crack the claws and serve on a warmed oval plate, garnished with lemon slices and parsley. Serve béarnaise sauce or beurre fondu separately.

Steamed Lobster

SERVES FOUR

4 lobsters, about 450–550 g (1–1¼ lb) each
Vinegar Court Bouillon (see page 88)
1 lemon and parsley sprigs, to garnish
225 g (8 oz) melted butter, to serve

A simple dish which brings out the fine, delicate taste of lobster perfectly. Serve with steamed potatoes and beurre fondu—melted butter flavoured with salt, pepper and lemon juice.

1. Put the lobsters into a steamer above a container of vinegar court bouillon. Cover and steam rapidly for about 15–20 minutes.

2. When cooked, split each lobster in half lengthways, remove the sac from the head and crack the claws to facilitate eating.

3. Arrange on a warmed oval plate, garnished with lemon and parsley. Serve the melted butter separately.

Spicy Crab Dip

SERVES FOUR

---

225 g (8 oz) cottage cheese

225 g (8 oz) white crab meat, flaked

45 ml (3 tbsp) canned pimiento, finely chopped

10 ml (2 tsp) Worcestershire sauce

5 ml (1 tsp) anchovy essence

2.5 ml (½ level tsp) cayenne pepper

juice of ½ lemon

salt and freshly ground pepper

sticks of raw celery, carrot and cucumber, cauliflower florets, spring onions and small whole radishes, to serve

---

Dips make informal starters or can be used to add interest to party fare. The raw vegetables used to dip, known as crudités, can be varied according to personal preference—try strips of red and green pepper, fennel or cherry tomatoes.

1. Press the cottage cheese through a sieve into a bowl. Fold the crab meat into the cottage cheese until evenly mixed.

2. Fold in the pimiento, then stir in the Worcestershire sauce, anchovy essence, half the cayenne, the lemon juice and salt and pepper to taste.

3. Turn the dip into a serving bowl, then sprinkle with the remaining cayenne. Chill for at least 2 hours. Serve the dip with a platter of raw vegetables.

Mussels with Garlic and Parsley

SERVES FOUR TO SIX

2.3 litres (4 pints) or 1.1–1.4 kg (2½–3 lb) mussels, prepared (see page 98)

150 ml (10 tbsp) fresh breadcrumbs

150 ml (10 tbsp) chopped fresh parsley

2 garlic cloves, skinned and finely chopped

freshly ground black pepper

100 ml (4 fl oz) olive oil

30 ml (2 tbsp) grated Parmesan cheese

lemon wedges, to serve

Many people associate mussels with the best French restaurants, but in fact they make quite an inexpensive starter. Be sure to use them on the day of purchase. Serve these mussels, coated in garlic-flavoured breadcrumbs, with French bread.

1. Place the mussels in a large saucepan with 1 cm (½ inch) water. Cover and cook over a high heat for 5–10 minutes until the mussels are open, shaking the pan frequently. Discard any mussels that do not open.

2. Shell the mussels, reserving one half of each empty shell. Strain the mussel liquid through a sieve lined with absorbent kitchen paper and reserve.

3. Mix together the breadcrumbs, parsley, garlic and plenty of pepper. Add the oil and 60 ml (4 tbsp) of the mussel liquid. Blend well together. Taste and adjust the seasonings.

4. Place the mussels in their shells on two baking sheets. With your fingers, pick up a good pinch of the breadcrumb mixture and press it down on each mussel, covering it well and filling the shell. Sprinkle with the Parmesan.

5. Bake in the oven at 230°C (450°F) mark 8 for 10 minutes, swapping the baking sheets over halfway through the cooking time. Serve with lemon wedges.

Opposite: Smoked Haddock Chowder (see page 79)
Overleaf: Chilled Smoked Trout with Yogurt and Orange Dressing (see page 79)

Mussels in White Wine

SERVES FOUR TO SIX

1 shallot, skinned and finely chopped
25 g (1 oz) celery, chopped
100 ml (4 fl oz) dry white wine
2.3 litres (4 pints) mussels, prepared (see page 98)
15 ml (1 tbsp) chopped fresh parsley
100 ml (4 fl oz) double cream
freshly ground pepper

An impressive start to a meal, this dish is quick and easy to prepare. After cooking in white wine, the mussels, on the half shell, are coated in a rich cream sauce. Accompany with warm crusty bread.

1. Put the shallot, celery and wine into a saucepan and bring to the boil. Add the mussels and cover the pan with a close fitting lid. Cook over a high heat for 5–10 minutes, shaking the pan frequently, until the mussel shells open.

2. Remove from the heat and discard any shells which have not opened. Take the one loose shell from each mussel and put the mussels on their shell into a warmed dish or individual cocottes. Keep warm.

3. Return the pan to the heat and add the parsley, cream and pepper to taste. Bring just to boiling point and pour the sauce over the mussels, being careful to leave behind any grit that may remain in the bottom of the pan. Serve immediately.

Oysters and Guinness Soup

SERVES FOUR

25 g (1 oz) butter
1 shallot, skinned and finely chopped
150 ml (¼ pint) dry white wine
1 quantity Fish Velouté (see page 89)
12 No. 2 oysters
300 ml (½ pint) Guinness
150 ml (¼ pint) double cream
15 ml (1 tbsp) chopped fresh parsley, to garnish

Wheeler's reputation was founded upon oysters, and here they are combined with one of the best known accompanying drinks, Guinness, in a superb soup.

1. Melt the butter in a saucepan, add the shallot and cook gently without colouring.

2. Add the wine, bring to the boil then stir in the velouté. Gradually bring to the boil and simmer for 15 minutes.

3. Open the oysters (see page 98) and add their liquor to the soup. Stir in the Guinness and bring back to almost boiling point, then pour in the cream. Strain through a fine strainer.

4. Gently reheat the soup and, just before serving, add the oysters. Serve in a warmed tureen with parsley sprinkled over.

Grilled Oysters

SERVES FOUR

12 rashers streaky bacon
24 oysters, opened (see page 98)
1 quantity Tarragon Butter Sauce (see page 89)
lemon wedges and fresh parsley sprigs, to garnish

Oysters have a natural affinity with bacon, which is often an ingredient in the oyster stews from America's eastern seaboard. This dish would make an impressive drinks' snack or after-dinner savoury.

1. Split each rasher lengthways in two.

2. Remove the oysters and wrap each in a strip of bacon. Secure the bacon with a wooden cocktail stick.

3. Cook under a preheated grill until the bacon is just cooked. Heat eight oyster shells.

4. Place some sauce on each shell, then top each with three oysters. Garnish with lemon and parsley. Serve immediately.

Overleaf: Lettuce Dolmas with Smoked Mackerel Filling (see page 83)
Opposite: Smoked Salmon and Trout Mousses (see page 83)

65

Oysters Au Gratin

SERVES SIX

50 g (2 oz) streaky bacon, finely chopped
75 g (3 oz) celery, trimmed and finely chopped
200 g (7 oz) can artichoke hearts, drained and finely chopped
12 large oysters
200 g (7 oz) Mozzarella cheese, thinly sliced

Flavoured with bacon and artichoke hearts, this mouthwatering oyster starter is grilled with cheese until golden. Italian Mozzarella is an excellent cheese to cook with.

1. In a small saucepan, fry the bacon until the fat begins to run. Add the celery and artichokes and cook, stirring, for 2–3 minutes. Cool.

2. Scrub the oyster shells well. Open the oysters (see page 98) and discard the flatter shells.

3. Spoon a little of the artichoke mixture over each oyster. Place slices of Mozzarella cheese on top. Cook under a preheated medium grill for about 20 minutes. The cheese will turn a deep golden and the oyster underneath will be cooked.

Prawns Fried in Garlic

SERVES TWO

50 g (2 oz) butter
30 ml (2 tbsp) olive oil
12 whole Dublin Bay prawns
3 garlic cloves, skinned and crushed
60 ml (4 tbsp) brandy
salt and freshly ground pepper
lemon wedges and shredded lettuce, to serve

Dublin Bay prawns, which are becoming increasingly available on fish stalls, are the variety to use in this spectacular dish. Small prawns could be used but the dish will just not look the same!

1. Melt the butter with the oil in a large heavy-based pan. Add the prawns (cook half at a time if your pan is not large enough) and the garlic and fry over high heat for 5 minutes, tossing the prawns constantly.

2. Sprinkle the brandy over the prawns with salt and pepper to taste. Serve immediately, garnished with lemon wedges and lettuce.

Potted Prawn Pâté

SERVES EIGHT

75 g (3 oz) butter, softened
10 ml (2 tsp) lemon juice
20 ml (4 tsp) chopped fresh parsley
salt and freshly ground pepper
175 g (6 oz) peeled prawns, finely chopped
whole prawns and lemon or lime slices, to garnish

A simple, speedy shellfish pâté to make for a light summer lunch or starter. Serve with crusty French bread or hot toast.

1. Beat 50 g (2 oz) of the butter with the lemon juice, parsley and salt and pepper to taste. Beat in the prawns.

2. Spoon into a serving dish and level the surface. Melt the remaining butter and pour over the prawn mixture.

3. Refrigerate for 1 hour. Garnish with prawns and lemon.

Malaysian-style Prawns

SERVES FOUR

30 ml (2 tbsp) vegetable oil
1 onion, skinned and very finely chopped
2 garlic cloves, skinned and crushed
2.5 cm (1 inch) piece fresh root ginger, skinned and crushed
2 dried red chillis, finely chopped
15 ml (1 level tbsp) ground coriander
10 ml (2 level tsp) turmeric
5 ml (1 level tsp) salt
700 g (1½ lb) peeled prawns
half a 200 g (7 oz) block creamed coconut, broken into pieces
juice of 1 lime or lemon
15–25 g (½–1 oz) coconut shreds or shredded coconut (optional)
lime or lemon slices, whole prawns (optional) and fresh coriander sprigs, to garnish

An exotic stir-fry dish that is quick to prepare. Creamed coconut, used to make coconut milk in the recipe, is sold in blocks in larger supermarkets, ethnic stores and delicatessens; it is more convenient to use than a fresh coconut.

1. Heat the oil in a wok or large frying pan, add the onion, garlic and ginger and fry gently for 5 minutes. Sprinkle in the chillis, spices and salt and stir-fry for 2–3 minutes more.

2. Add the prawns to the pan and stir-fry for 5 minutes until heated through and evenly coated in the spice mixture.

3. Crumble in the coconut, then gradually add about 300 ml (½ pint) boiling water (just enough to make a thick gravy that coats the prawns). Bring to the boil, stirring all the time, then simmer for 5 minutes, stirring frequently. Taste and add salt, if necessary.

4. Transfer to a warmed serving dish and squeeze the juice from the lime evenly over the top. Sprinkle with the coconut shreds, if used, then garnish with lime or lemon slices, whole prawns, if used, and coriander. Serve immediately.

Melon and Prawn Salad

SERVES EIGHT

1 small honeydew melon, halved and seeded
30 ml (2 tbsp) tomato juice
30 ml (2 tbsp) cider vinegar
30 ml (2 tbsp) clear honey
1 egg yolk
450 g (1 lb) peeled prawns
225 g (8 oz) cucumber, diced
15 ml (1 tbsp) chopped fresh tarragon or 5 ml (1 level tsp) dried
salt and freshly ground pepper
tarragon sprigs and 8 large whole prawns, to garnish

The unusual combination of shellfish and melon in a piquant herb dressing provides a refreshing new starter idea. The popular honeydew melon is used here. To test for the correct degree of ripeness, press gently at both ends of the melon; the skin should give slightly under pressure of your thumb.

1. Scoop out the melon flesh with a melon baller. Divide the melon balls equally between eight individual serving dishes.

2. Put the tomato juice, vinegar, honey and egg yolk in a blender or food processor and blend together until evenly mixed.

3. Toss the prawns, cucumber and tarragon in the tomato dressing. Add salt and pepper to taste.

4. Spoon on top of the melon balls and chill for at least 1 hour. Garnish with sprigs of tarragon and whole prawns before serving.

Skewered Prawns with Garlic Butter

SERVES FOUR

16 raw Pacific prawns or Dublin Bay prawn tails
12 fresh bay leaves
75 g (3 oz) butter
3 large garlic cloves, skinned and crushed
15 ml (1 tbsp) chopped fresh oregano or 5 ml (1 level tsp) dried
30 ml (2 tbsp) lemon juice
salt and freshly ground pepper
30 ml (2 tbsp) chopped fresh parsley, to serve
lemon or lime wedges, to serve

These large succulent prawns make a luxurious starter for a special occasion. It is essential to buy really large prawns for this dish, usually only available from a good fishmonger. If your fishmonger sells 'jumbo' or 'Mediterranean' prawns, these are also suitable.

1. Remove the legs and, with a sharp knife, make a slit down the centre of the back and remove the intestinal vein. Wash well.

2. Thread the prawns and bay leaves on to four skewers and place in a single layer on a well-oiled grill pan.

3. Melt the butter in a saucepan, add the garlic and fry gently until golden. Remove from the heat and stir in the oregano, lemon juice and salt and pepper to taste.

4. Pour the garlic butter over the prawns, turning them to coat well. Cook under a preheated grill for 5–8 minutes until the prawns turn pink.

5. Arrange on a warmed serving platter, pour over the pan juices and sprinkle with chopped parsley. Serve hot, with lemon wedges.

Prawn and Dill Tartlets

MAKES SIX

175 g (6 oz) Shortcrust Pastry (see page 93)
50 g (2 oz) spring onions, trimmed and finely chopped
2 egg yolks
200 ml (7 fl oz) double cream
2.5 ml (½ tsp) chopped fresh dill or 1.25 ml (¼ level tsp) dried
salt and freshly ground pepper
36 peeled prawns
6 whole prawns, to garnish

Savoury tartlets make filling starters, so serve when a light main course is to follow. Garnishing with whole unshelled prawns gives a sophisticated finishing touch.

1. Roll out the pastry thinly and use to line six individual fluted flan dishes. Bake the pastry 'blind' in the oven at 200°C (400°F) mark 6 for 15 minutes until just set and beginning to colour.

2. Divide the spring onions between the flan dishes. In a bowl, mix together the egg yolks, cream, dill and salt and pepper to taste. Pour into the cases to fill two-thirds deep. Arrange the peeled prawns in the custard mixture.

3. Reduce the oven temperature to 170°C (325°F) mark 3 and bake the tartlets for 20 minutes until set.

4. Serve warm, not hot, garnished with the whole prawns.

Prawn Risotto

SERVES FOUR

1 small onion, skinned and thinly sliced
1 garlic clove, skinned and crushed
1 litre (1¾ pints) light stock
225 g (8 oz) long grain brown rice
50 g (2 oz) small button mushrooms
½ sachet saffron threads
225 g (8 oz) peeled prawns
50 g (2 oz) petits pois

This satisfying shellfish risotto needs only a refreshing tomato salad to accompany it. Nutritious brown rice, with its chewy texture and nutty flavour, is used in this recipe.

1. Place the onion, garlic, stock, rice, mushrooms and saffron in a large saucepan or flameproof casserole. Add salt and pepper to taste. Bring to the boil and simmer, uncovered, for 35 minutes, stirring occasionally.

2. Stir in the prawns and petits pois. Cook over high heat for about 5 minutes, stirring occasionally until most of the liquid has been absorbed.

3. Taste and adjust the seasoning, then turn into a warmed serving dish. Garnish with whole prawns, if liked, and serve immediately.

Scallops in Vermouth

SERVES FOUR

selection of salad vegetables such as endive, chicory, lamb's tongue lettuce, watercress etc.
60 ml (4 tbsp) sunflower oil
1 garlic clove, skinned and crushed
700 g (1½ lb) large shelled scallops, prepared
10 ml (2 tsp) white wine vinegar
60 ml (4 tbsp) dry vermouth
salt and freshly ground pepper

One of the prettiest of shellfish, fresh scallops are sold in or out of their delicately coloured, fan-shaped shells. When buying the green salad for this special occasion starter, choose some of the less familiar salad vegetables.

1. Line a large serving dish with the salad ingredients. Cover and refrigerate.

2. Heat the oil in a medium saucepan, add the garlic and lightly fry for 1–2 minutes. Add the scallops, vinegar and vermouth. Simmer, uncovered, over a moderate heat for about 10 minutes until the sauce is smooth and syrupy. Add salt and pepper to taste.

3. Remove the scallops with a slotted spoon and thinly slice. Return to the pan. Leave to cool slightly before spooning into the salad-lined dish. Serve immediately.

Scallops au Gratin

SERVES FOUR

8 large scallops
1 quantity Sauce Duxelles (see page 90)
60 ml (4 tbsp) dry white wine
salt and freshly ground pepper
100 g (4 oz) mushrooms, wiped and sliced
175 g (6 oz) white breadcrumbs
100 g (4 oz) butter, melted
juice of 1 lemon
lemon slices and parsley sprigs, to garnish

The shells of large scallops can be as large as 15 cm (6 inches), while those of the smaller queen and bay scallops are usually about 5 cm (2 inches); use large ones for this recipe.

1. Open the shells and remove the scallops (see page 98).

2. Scrub eight of the shells. Coat the bases with a little Duxelles sauce, then with white wine. Lay the white of the scallop in the shell and put the orange coral on top. Season.

Surround with slices of mushrooms and cover with more sauce.

3. Sprinkle with the breadcrumbs and melted butter. Bake in the oven at 200°C (400°F) mark 6 for about 10–15 minutes.

4. When cooked, sprinkle with a little lemon juice. Garnish and serve on a warmed platter.

Scallops in Creamy Basil Sauce

SERVES FOUR

30 ml (2 tbsp) vegetable oil
15 g (½ oz) butter
1 small onion, skinned and finely chopped
2 garlic cloves, skinned and crushed
900 g (2 lb) shelled scallops, cut into fairly thick slices
150 ml (¼ pint) dry white wine
20 ml (4 tsp) chopped fresh basil
salt and freshly ground pepper
150 ml (¼ pint) double cream
few fresh basil sprigs, to garnish

Scallops are amongst the dearest of shellfish. To make a less expensive, and lighter, lunch or supper dish, halve the quantity of scallops and replace with 450 g (1 lb) white button mushrooms.

1. Heat the oil and butter in a large frying pan, add the onion and garlic and fry gently for 5 minutes until soft and lightly coloured.

2. Add the scallops to the pan and toss to coat in the oil and butter. Stir in the wine, basil and salt and pepper to taste.

3. Fry the scallops over a moderate heat for 10 minutes until they are tender, turning them constantly so that they cook evenly on all sides. Do not overcook or they will become tough and rubbery.

4. Remove the scallops from the liquid with a slotted spoon and set aside on a plate. Boil the liquid until reduced by about half, then stir in the cream a little at a time and simmer until the sauce is thick.

5. Return the scallops to the pan and heat gently. Taste and adjust the seasoning and serve garnished with basil sprigs.

Scampi Provençale

SERVES FOUR

salt and freshly ground pepper
40 shelled scampi
50 g (2 oz) plain flour
75 ml (3 fl oz) olive oil
1 garlic clove, skinned and crushed
1 quantity Tomato Sauce (see page 90)
chopped fresh parsley, to garnish

In this elegant main course dish, the fine rich flavour of scampi is complemented by a sauce made with fresh tomatoes. Serve with plain boiled rice and a tossed green salad.

1. Sprinkle salt and pepper to taste over the scampi. Coat in the flour, shaking off any excess.

2. Heat the oil in a frying pan and lightly fry the garlic and scampi, until the scampi are coloured on each side. Drain off the oil.

3. Stir in the tomato sauce. Bring to the boil and simmer gently for 10 minutes. Adjust the seasoning if necessary.

4. Place in a warmed serving dish and sprinkle with chopped parsley.

Scampi Brochettes

SERVES FOUR

1 quantity Fish Marinade (see page 88)
40 shelled scampi
lemon slices and parsley sprigs, to garnish
1 quantity Tarragon Butter Sauce, to serve (see page 89)

Succulent scampi, one of the smaller members of the lobster family, are unusual in that they are pink before cooking. Here they are marinated in a lemon, olive oil and herb marinade, then grilled.

1. Pour the marinade into a shallow dish. Arrange the scampi on four skewers and put into the marinade for about 2 hours, turning from time to time.

2. Remove the scampi from the marinade and drain. Cook under a preheated grill, turning frequently, for 5–10 minutes.

3. Garnish and serve on a warmed platter. Serve the sauce separately.

Squid in White Wine

SERVES FOUR

1 kg (2¼ lb) small squid

75 ml (5 tbsp) olive oil

salt and freshly ground pepper

75 ml (3 fl oz) dry white wine

2 garlic cloves, skinned and crushed

juice of ½ lemon

15 ml (1 tbsp) chopped fresh parsley

Armed with a sac of ink which they squirt out when threatened by an enemy, squid need to be prepared and skinned before use (see page 100). They make an unusual and interesting meal. Serve this fish stew Italian style—with rice or toast.

1. Cut the squid bodies into 5 mm (¼ inch) rings. Place in a bowl with the tentacles and spoon over 45 ml (3 tbsp) of the oil with plenty of salt and pepper to taste. Leave for 3 hours.

2. Pour the squid and marinade into a large frying pan and cook for 5 minutes, turning frequently. Add the wine and garlic and cook for a further 5 minutes. Add the ink sacs, breaking them up with a spoon.

3. Cover and cook over a low heat for about 40 minutes until the squid is tender.

4. Add the remaining oil, the lemon juice and parsley. Stir for 3 minutes over a high heat, adjust the seasoning and serve.

Squid Salad with Prawns

SERVES EIGHT TO TEN

1.1–1.4 kg (2½–3 lb) squid, prepared and skinned (see page 100)

6 garlic cloves, skinned and crushed with 5 ml (1 tsp) salt

300 ml (½ pint) full-bodied Italian red wine

½ onion, skinned and finely sliced

1 red pepper, cored, seeded and thinly sliced

1 green pepper, cored, seeded and thinly sliced

135 ml (9 tbsp) olive oil

juice of 1 lemon

700 g (1½ lb) whole prawns or 225 g (8 oz) peeled prawns and 12 whole prawns, to garnish

one 50 g (2 oz) can anchovies in oil, drained and soaked in milk for 20 minutes

15 ml (1 tbsp) chopped fresh basil, or 10 ml (2 level tsp) dried

freshly ground pepper

few large lettuce leaves

fresh basil sprigs and black olives, to garnish

This mixed seafood salad is a special occasion starter. The squid is first cooked in red wine, then mixed with prawns and anchovies.

1. Cut the body of the squid into thin rings, reserving the tentacles. Cut these into small pieces. If they are very small, leave some whole.

2. Put all the squid pieces in an ovenproof dish. Add half the garlic, pour over the wine and 300 ml (½ pint) water. Cover and cook in the oven at 180°C (350°F) mark 4 for 1½–2 hours until tender. Cool.

3. Drain the squid, then rinse quickly under cold running water and drain again thoroughly. Put into a bowl with the remaining garlic, the onion, red and green peppers, olive oil and lemon juice. Stir well to mix.

4. Peel the prawns, if using whole prawns, reserving twelve whole ones for the garnish. Drain the anchovies, rinse and pat dry on

absorbent kitchen paper, then chop them roughly.

5. Add the peeled prawns to the salad with the anchovies, basil and pepper to taste. Fold gently to mix, then cover and leave to stand for about 1 hour.

6. To serve, line a bowl with lettuce leaves and pile the squid and prawns into the centre. Garnish with the reserved whole prawns, basil sprigs and black olives.

Creamy Shellfish Dip

SERVES SIX TO EIGHT

350 g (12 oz) crab meat, flaked
275 g (10 oz) peeled shrimps
450 g (1 lb) full-fat soft cheese
60 ml (4 tbsp) creamed horseradish
finely grated rind and juice of 1 lemon
5 ml (1 level tsp) paprika
freshly ground pepper
lemon slices, to garnish

Crab meat and shrimps combine with soft cheese to make a rich, creamy dip, spiked with the flavour of horseradish. Serve at a drinks party with plenty of crudités and savoury biscuits to dip.

1. Mix the crab meat and shrimps in a blender or food processor until the flesh is broken down to a pulp.

2. Add the soft cheese in batches and blend until evenly combined with the fish. When all the cheese is incorporated, add the creamed horseradish, lemon rind and juice, paprika and pepper and blend well.

3. Turn the mixture into serving bowls and sprinkle black pepper liberally over the surface. Garnish with lemon slices and chill until required.

Italian Seafood Salad

SERVES SIX

1.1 litres (2 pints) mussels, prepared and cooked, with cooking liquid reserved (see page 98)
1 onion, skinned and roughly chopped
1 bay leaf
salt and freshly ground pepper
350 g (12 oz) squid, cleaned (see page 100)
350 g (12 oz) shelled scallops
350 g (12 oz) peeled prawns
1 small green pepper, cored, seeded and finely sliced into strips
1 small red pepper, cored, seeded and finely sliced into strips
1 carrot, peeled and shredded into ribbons
150 ml (¼ pint) olive oil
60 ml (4 tbsp) lemon juice
30 ml (2 tbsp) capers
45 ml (3 tbsp) chopped fresh parsley
1 garlic clove, skinned and crushed
black olives, to garnish

All the fish and shellfish specified in this Italian recipe are available at most good fishmongers, but if you have difficulty in obtaining one particular kind it will not spoil the dish to leave it out. Serve as part of a classic Italian dinner party.

1. In a large saucepan, mix together the cooking liquid from the mussels and 1.75 litres (3 pints) water. Add the onion, bay leaf and a pinch of salt and bring to the boil. Add the squid and simmer gently for 20 minutes or until tender.

2. Remove the squid from the cooking liquid and set aside.

3. Bring the liquid back to the boil, add the scallops and poach gently for 3 minutes. Remove the scallops from the liquid with a slotted spoon and set aside. (Reserve the fish liquid for making a soup.)

4. Using a sharp knife, cut the squid into rings approximately 1 cm (½ inch) wide.

5. Cut the scallops into four, removing the tough muscle (found near the coral or roe).

6. Reserve a few mussels in their shells for garnish. Remove the shells from the remaining mussels and put the mussels in a large serving bowl with the squid, prawns and scallops. Add the peppers and carrot.

7. Mix together the oil, lemon juice, capers, parsley and garlic—with pepper to taste. Pour over the seafood. Mix lightly but thoroughly. Taste and add salt if necessary.

8. Chill for at least 2 hours and then serve garnished with black olives and the reserved mussels in shells.

Opposite: Hot crab and Ricotta Quiche (see page 61)
Overleaf: Steamed Lobster (see page 63)

Oriental Seafood Salad

SERVES FOUR

30 ml (2 tbsp) sesame oil
½ small onion, peeled and very finely chopped
2.5 cm (1 inch) fresh root ginger, peeled and grated
10 ml (2 tsp) soy sauce, ot to taste
120 ml (8 tbsp) thick Mayonnaise (see page 91)
275 g (10 oz) white crab meat, flaked
175 g (6 oz) peeled prawns
1 red pepper, cored, seeded and diced
¼ cucumber, diced
50 g (2 oz) fresh beansprouts
few Chinese leaves or lettuce leaves, shredded
juice of 1 lime

The perfect starter to an eastern style main course. Prawns and crab meat are added to this crunchy salad while lime juice provides the tangy flavour.

1. Heat the oil in a small saucepan, add the onion and ginger and fry gently until soft. Remove from the heat, transfer to a large bowl and leave to cool.

2. Stir in the soy sauce and mayonnaise, with salt and pepper to taste.

3. Fold the crab meat and prawns gently into the mayonnaise mixture, then fold in the red pepper, cucumber and beansprouts. Adjust

seasoning, remembering that soy sauce is quite salty.

4. Line four glass dishes with the Chinese leaves or lettuce. Pile the seafood cocktail in the centre, then squeeze a little lime juice over each serving. Garnish with lime slices and whole prawns, if liked.

Seafood Saffron Risotto

SERVES FOUR TO SIX

good pinch of saffron strands
45 ml (3 tbsp) olive oil
30 ml (2 tbsp) butter
1 onion, skinned and chopped
2 garlic cloves, skinned and crushed
½ green pepper, cored, seeded and finely chopped
½ red pepper, cored, seeded and finely chopped
400 g (14 oz) Italian risotto rice
about 600 ml (1 pint) hot Fish Stock (see page 88)
120 ml (8 tbsp) dry white wine
1 bay leaf
salt and freshly ground pepper
350–450 g (12 oz–1 lb) peeled scampi or jumbo prawns
24 cooked mussels, shelled (see page 98)
a few mussels in shells, to garnish
freshly grated Parmesan cheese, to serve

This golden risotto with succulent scampi uses Italian risotto rice, also called *avorio* or *arborio*. It produces a creamy and moist consistency where the grains of rice stick together.

1. Soak the saffron strands in 150 ml (¼ pint) boiling water for at least 30 minutes.

2. Meanwhile, heat the oil and half the butter in a heavy-based saucepan, add the onion, garlic and peppers and fry gently for 5 minutes until soft.

3. Add the rice and stir until well coated. Pour in a few spoonfuls of the stock and the wine, then add the saffron liquid.

4. Add the bay leaf and salt and pepper to taste and simmer gently, stirring frequently, until all the liquid is absorbed by the rice.

5. Add a few more spoonfuls of stock and simmer again until absorbed. Continue adding stock in this way for about 15 minutes, stirring frequently until the rice is *al dente*.

6. Melt the remaining butter in a separate pan, add the scampi and toss gently for about 5 minutes until they change colour.

7. Remove the bay leaf from the risotto, then stir in the scampi and juices and the mussels. Warm through, taste and adjust seasoning. Turn into a warmed serving dish. Top with whole mussels and serve at once with grated Parmesan cheese handed separately.

Overleaf: Mussels with Garlic and Parsley (see page 64)
Opposite: Potted Prawn Paté (see page 66)

Seafood Pilaff

SERVES FOUR

225 g (8 oz) tomatoes, skinned, seeded and quartered, reserving juices
50 g (2 oz) butter
1 small onion, skinned and sliced
175 g (6 oz) long grain rice
2.5 ml (½ level tsp) turmeric
5 ml (1 level tsp) paprika
300 ml (½ pint) light stock
1 green pepper, cored, seeded and diced
1 garlic clove, skinned and crushed
15 ml (1 tbsp) tomato purée
salt and freshly ground pepper
100 g (4 oz) peeled prawns
100 g (4 oz) white crab meat, flaked
100 g (4 oz) cooked mussels, in their shells
30 ml (2 tbsp) medium sherry

This mixed shellfish rice dish looks attractive served on natural scallop shells placed on serving plates. Newly acquired scallop shells must first be scrubbed then sterilised in boiling water before use.

1. Cut each tomato quarter in half lengthways, again reserving any juices.

2. Melt the butter in a medium flameproof casserole, add the onion and cook until brown. Stir in the rice with the turmeric and paprika and cook gently for 1 minute. Stir in the stock, green pepper, garlic, tomato purée and salt and pepper to taste. Bring to the boil.

3. Cover the dish tightly and cook in the oven at 170°C (325°F) mark 3 for 20 minutes.

4. Remove from the oven and stir in the prawns, crab and mussels with the tomatoes

and their juices and sherry, mixing well. Cover again and return to the oven for a further 10–15 minutes or until all the liquid has been absorbed and the rice is tender. Adjust seasoning and serve hot.

La Mouclade

SERVES FOUR

2.3 litres (4 pints) or 1.1–1.4 kg (2½–3 lb) mussels, prepared (see page 98)
150 ml (¼ pint) dry white wine
½ small onion, skinned and finely chopped
25 g (1 oz) butter
2 garlic cloves, skinned and crushed
15 g (½ oz) plain flour
300 ml (½ pint) double cream
pinch of saffron or turmeric powder
30 ml (2 tbsp) lemon juice
freshly ground pepper
1 egg yolk
chopped fresh parsley, to garnish

There is never any need to worry about mussels these days, as long as you buy them from a reputable fishmonger. All mussels offered for sale must, by law, undergo a special cleaning process, so there is absolutely no risk of shellfish poisoning. Always be sure to cook the mussels on the day of purchase, however, and to clean and cook them correctly (see page 98).

1. Place the mussels in a large saucepan. Pour in the wine and add the chopped onion, cover and cook over high heat for 5–10 minutes until the mussels are open, shaking the pan frequently.

2. Pour through a sieve, reserving the

cooking liquid. Discard one half shell from each mussel. Keep the mussels warm.

3. Make the sauce. Boil the cooking liquid rapidly until reduced by half. Melt the butter in a saucepan, add the garlic and fry gently for 1 minute. Add the flour and cook gently, stirring, for 1–2 minutes. Gradually blend in the reduced cooking liquid. Bring to the boil, stirring constantly, add the cream and saffron or turmeric and simmer for 3 minutes until slightly thickened and smooth. Add the lemon juice and pepper to taste.

4. Remove the pan from the heat and stir in the egg yolk. Pour the sauce over the mussels, sprinkle with parsley and serve.

Dressed Crab

SERVES TWO TO THREE

shell and meat from 1 medium (900 g / 2 lb) cooked crab (to remove the crab meat and prepare the shell, see page 99)
salt and freshly ground pepper
15 ml (1 tbsp) lemon juice
30 ml (2 tbsp) fresh white breadcrumbs
1 egg, hard-boiled
chopped fresh parsley
lettuce or endive, to serve

Serve this delicious summertime lunch dish with a fresh tomato salad.

1. Using two forks, flake all the white meat from the crab, removing any shell or membrane. Season, adding about 5 ml (1 tsp) lemon juice.

2. Pound the brown meat and work in the breadcrumbs with the remaining lemon juice and seasoning.

3. Using a small spoon, put the white meat in both ends of the crab's empty shell, making sure that it is well piled up into the shell. Keep the inside edges neat.

4. Then spoon the brown meat in a neat line down the centre, between the two sections of white crab meat.

5. Chop the egg white. Sieve the yolk.

6. Hold a blunt knife between the white and brown crab meat and carefully spoon lines of parsley, sieved egg yolk and chopped egg white across the crab, moving the knife as you go to keep a neat edge. Serve the filled shell on a bed of lettuce or endive, surrounded by the small legs.

SMOKED FISH

*B*efore the days of refrigeration, fish was cured and smoked to preserve it. Today, smoking is used to create flavour rather than to improve the keeping qualities.

There are two basic ways of smoking fish, cold-smoking and hot-smoking. Whichever process is used, the fish is first salted or brined (this gives the finished fish its glossy appearance). It is then drained, hung on racks in a kiln and exposed to smoke from burning wood or peat for 5–6 hours.

In cold-smoking, the fish is cured by smoking in a temperature no higher than 33°C (91°F) to avoid cooking it. With the exception of smoked salmon, all cold-smoked fish requires cooking.

In hot-smoking, the fish is smoked at a temperature of 70–80°C (158–176°F) at some stage during the process to cook the flesh. Hot-smoked fish does not require further cooking. Check with your fishmonger, or the packet instructions, to tell which smoking process has been used.

The range of fish which can be smoked is fairly wide, although oily fish are most suitable. Smoked fish include the various smoked herrings (kippers, bloaters, buckling and sprats); smoked haddock (Finnan haddock, Arbroath smokies, fillets and golden cutlets), as well as salmon, trout, eel, mackerel and cod's roe.

RECISPES

Smoked Haddock with Cream and Pernod

SERVES FOUR

4 smoked haddock fillets, about 700 g (1½ lb) total weight
300 ml (½ pint) milk
1 very small onion, skinned and sliced
2 bay leaves
few black peppercorns
2.5 ml (½ level tsp) crushed fennel seeds
150 ml (¼ pint) double cream
15 g (½ oz) butter
60 ml (4 tbsp) Pernod
salt and freshly ground pepper
fennel sprigs, to garnish

This rich and unusual dinner party main course needs only plain rice or boiled new potatoes to accompany it. Half the recipe amount will make a filling starter, but the main dish should then be fairly simple.

1. Put the smoked haddock fillets in a large flameproof casserole. Pour in the milk and add the onion slices, bay leaves, peppercorns and fennel seeds. Pour in a little water if the liquid does not completely cover the smoked haddock.

2. Bring slowly to boiling point, then lower the heat, cover and simmer gently for 15 minutes or until the fish flakes easily when tested with a fork.

3. Remove the fish fillets from the cooking liquid and then carefully flake the flesh into chunky pieces. Discard the skin and any bones.

4. Strain the cooking liquid and return to the rinsed-out pan. Bring to the boil and boil to reduce slightly, then add the cream, butter and Pernod. Heat again until the sauce thickens.

5. Return the fish to the liquid and heat through. Add salt and pepper to taste (taking care not to add too much salt as the fish is salty), then transfer to a warmed serving dish. Garnish with fennel sprigs and serve immediately.

Smoked Haddock and Prawn Lasagne

SERVES FOUR

175 g (6 oz) lasagne
15 ml (1 tbsp) vegetable oil
450 g (1 lb) smoked haddock fillet, skinned
198 g (7 oz) can sweetcorn
50 g (2 oz) butter
1 small onion, skinned and finely chopped
45 ml (3 level tbsp) plain flour
568 ml (1 pint) milk
salt and freshly ground pepper
75 g (3 oz) peeled prawns
50 g (2 oz) Cheddar cheese, grated

The unusual combination of smoked haddock and prawns combines well in this filling pasta dish. This lasagne can be prepared in advance and refrigerated until required for baking.

1. Cook the lasagne in a large saucepan in plenty of boiling salted water, adding the oil to help prevent sticking. Drain well and put on a clean tea towel to dry.

2. Cut the haddock into small fork-size pieces. Drain the sweetcorn, reserving the liquid.

3. Melt the butter in a medium pan, add the onion and fry until soft. Stir in the flour, milk, 300 ml (½ pint) water and the liquid from the drained sweetcorn. Bring to the boil and add salt and pepper to taste.

4. Layer the sauce, lasagne, fish, sweetcorn and prawns in a 2.3 litre (4 pint) shallow ovenproof dish, starting and finishing with sauce. Make sure the sauce covers the pasta. Sprinkle over the cheese and cover with foil.

5. Bake in the oven at 180°C (350°F) mark 4 for 1 hour. Remove the foil, then put under a preheated hot grill to brown.

Smoked Haddock Chowder

SERVES FOUR

450 g (1 lb) smoked haddock fillet
50 g (2 oz) butter
1 large onion, skinned and sliced
30 ml (2 level tbsp) plain flour
225 g (8 oz) potatoes, peeled and cut into 1 cm (½ inch) cubes
175 g (6 oz) carrots, peeled and coarsely grated
150 ml (¼ pint) single cream
salt and freshly ground pepper
chopped fresh parsley, to garnish

Haddock, a smaller member of the cod family, is a fine tasting white fish that really comes into its own when smoked. Here it adds body and flavour to this chunky fish chowder, which can be served as a lunch or supper dish.

1. Put the haddock in a saucepan containing 1.1 litres (2 pints) water and simmer for 10 minutes until tender. Drain, reserving the liquid. Flake the flesh coarsely, discarding the skin and any bones.

2. Melt the butter in a saucepan, add the onion and fry until soft. Stir in the flour. Gradually add the strained fish stock and bring to the boil, stirring. Add the potatoes and carrots. Simmer for about 10 minutes until the vegetables are tender.

3. Stir in the cream and flaked fish. Add salt and pepper to taste. Heat through but do not boil. Garnish with chopped parsley.

Smoked Haddock Kedgeree

SERVES FOUR

175 g (6 oz) long grain brown rice
salt and freshly ground pepper
275 g (10 oz) smoked haddock
25 g (1 oz) butter
1 hard-boiled egg, chopped
30 ml (2 tbsp) chopped fresh parsley
juice of ½ lemon

This is a traditional breakfast dish, but also makes a tasty lunch or supper meal. The rice and smoked haddock can be cooked the day before, then heated through with the remaining ingredients in the morning at breakfast time.

1. Place the rice in a large saucepan of boiling salted water and cook for about 35 minutes, or according to packet instructions, until tender.

2. Meanwhile, place the haddock in a pan, cover with water and poach for about 15 minutes. Drain the fish well, then flake the flesh, discarding the skin and bones.

3. Drain the rice well. Melt the butter in a frying pan, add the rice, haddock, egg and parsley and stir over moderate heat for a few minutes until warmed through. Add the lemon juice and salt and pepper to taste, turn into a warmed serving dish and serve.

Chilled Smoked Trout with Yogurt and Orange Dressing

SERVES FOUR

4 small smoked trout, skinned and filleted
finely grated rind and juice of 1 orange
150 ml (¼ pint) natural yogurt
5 ml (1 tsp) creamed horseradish sauce
finely shredded lettuce or chicory leaves, to serve
orange segments, to garnish

Smoked trout is widely available at delicatessens and in most larger supermarkets. Serve as a light summer lunch with brown bread, or as a starter.

1. Cover the smoked trout fillets and chill for 30 minutes.

2. Meanwhile, mix the orange rind, juice, yogurt and horseradish together. Add salt and pepper to taste. Chill for at least 30 minutes with the smoked trout.

3. Cover four small serving plates with shredded lettuce or chicory. Carefully lay two fillets on each plate and spoon over the dressing. Garnish with orange segments and serve immediately.

Smoked Trout Mille-feuille

SERVES SIX

100 g (4 oz) Rough Puff Pastry (see page 92)

beaten egg, to glaze

15 ml (1 tbsp) black peppercorns, crushed

30 ml (2 tbsp) capers

198 g (7 oz) can sweetcorn kernels, drained

1 small smoked trout, about 225 g (8 oz)

150 ml (¼ pint) soured cream

5 ml (1 tsp) lemon juice

salt and freshly ground pepper

10 ml (2 level tsp) powdered gelatine

lemon wedges, to serve

This delightful layered fish and pastry dish should not be made up more than 2 hours before serving.

1. Thinly roll out the pastry to a rectangle 30.5 × 23 cm (12 × 9 inches). Cut into three 10 cm (4 inch) wide strips. Place the strips on a wetted baking sheet. Prick all over with a fork. Chill for 10 minutes.

2. Glaze the pastry strips with beaten egg. Sprinkle the peppercorns over one strip.

3. Bake in the oven at 200°C (400°F) mark 6 for 12–15 minutes or until golden. Cool.

4. Roughly chop the capers and drained sweetcorn. Flake the trout. Mix with the soured cream and lemon juice. Add salt and pepper to taste.

5. Place 30 ml (2 tbsp) very hot water in a bowl and sprinkle in the gelatine. Stir briskly until dissolved. Leave to cool, then stir into the fish mixture. Chill until beginning to set.

6. Layer the pastry and fish mixture, topping with the peppered pastry strip. Chill again until just set, at least 30 minutes. Serve thickly sliced with lemon wedges.

Smoked Trout Mousse in Lemon Shells

SERVES SIX

1 smoked trout, about 225 g (8 oz), skinned and boned

6 large, even-sized lemons

300 ml (½ pint) milk

few slices each of onion and carrot

1 bay leaf

4–6 peppercorns

7.5 ml (1½ tsp) powdered gelatine

25 g (1 oz) butter

30 ml (2 level tbsp) plain flour

90 ml (6 tbsp) double or whipping cream

15 ml (1 tbsp) creamed horseradish

1 egg white

salt and freshly ground pepper

chopped fresh parsley and fresh herb sprigs, to serve

The mousses may be served in individual ramekins, if preferred, and garnished with lemon butterflies.

1. Flake the trout flesh, discarding any remaining bones. Cover and set aside.

2. Cut the lemons in half lengthways and scoop out all the flesh and membranes with a sharp-edged teaspoon; reserve the shells. Measure 60 ml (4 tbsp) lemon juice, pour into a small heatproof bowl and reserve.

3. Bring the milk to the boil in a saucepan with the onion, carrot, bay leaf and peppercorns. Remove from the heat, cover and leave to infuse.

4. Sprinkle the gelatine over the reserved 60 ml (4 tbsp) lemon juice. Leave for 5 minutes until spongy, then stand the bowl in a pan of gently simmering water and heat until dissolved.

5. Melt the butter in a separate saucepan, add the flour and cook gently, stirring, for 1–2 minutes. Remove from the heat and gradually blend in the infused milk. Bring to the boil, stirring constantly, then simmer for 2 minutes. Turn into a bowl and stir in the liquid gelatine. Leave to cool.

6. Whip the cream and fold into the cold sauce with the horseradish and flaked trout. Whisk the egg white until stiff, then fold in gently until evenly incorporated. Add salt and pepper to taste, taking care not to add too much salt.

7. Spoon the mousse into the hollowed-out lemon shells, then chill for at least 4 hours or overnight if more convenient.

8. To serve, arrange two lemon shells on each of six serving plates, garnished with chopped parsley and a sprig of herbs. Serve chilled.

Pâté of Smoked Trout with Whiting

SERVES FOUR,

350 g (12 oz) smoked trout fillets, skinned
300 g (10 oz) whiting fillets, skinned
3 egg whites
600 ml (1 pint) double cream
salt and white pepper
lettuce leaves, lemon slices, tomato slices, radishes and parsley sprigs, to garnish
1 quantity Horseradish Mayonnaise (see page 91)

This creamy, mixed smoked and white fish pâté serves four as a main course or provides eight elegant starters.

1. Reserve two fillets of smoked trout. Purée the whiting fillets in a blender or food processor. Add the remainder of the smoked trout and purée, gradually adding the egg whites until all are incorporated.

2. Pass the mixture through a fine sieve and chill for 2 hours.

3. Beat the cream into the fish, a little at a time, until well blended. Add salt and pepper.

4. Butter a 0.75 litre (1¼ pint) terrine or other deep, lidded dish about 23 × 7.5 cm (9 × 3 inches) and put a layer of the mixture in the bottom filling about one-third of the dish. Lay the reserved fillets of smoked trout lengthways along the top, leaving a space between them. Fill the terrine with the remaining mixture and level the top.

5. Cover with greased greaseproof paper or foil and then the lid. Place the terrine in a roasting tin with water to come half way up the sides. Cook in the oven at 200°C (400°F) mark 6 for about 35–40 minutes.

6. To test if the pâté is cooked, insert a skewer into the centre of the pâté, remove and place the skewer point on the back of the hand. If it is hot, the pâté is cooked.

7. When cooked, remove from the roasting tin, remove the lid and place a light weight on top of the pâté while it cools. This will ensure an even textured pâté. When cold, refrigerate for at least 12 hours.

8. To serve, cut into slices approximately 1 cm (½ inch) thick and arrange on a medium plate garnished with lettuce, lemon, tomato, radish and parsley. Serve the horseradish mayonnaise separately.

Smoked Trout With Tomatoes and Mushrooms

SERVES EIGHT

700 g (1½ lb) smoked trout, skinned and boned
225 g (8 oz) cucumber, skinned and finely chopped
salt and freshly ground pepper
175 g (6 oz) mushrooms, wiped and finely chopped
45 ml (3 tbsp) creamed horseradish
30 ml (2 tbsp) lemon juice
60 ml (4 tbsp) natural yogurt
4 very large Marmande or Beefsteak tomatoes, about 350 g (12 oz) each, skinned
spring onion tops, snipped, to garnish

Serve as an impressive dinner party starter or as a light lunch with brown rolls. It is important to buy the very large continental-type tomatoes for this recipe. Choose ones that are not too misshapen or they will not sandwich together.

1. Flake the trout flesh. Sprinkle the cucumber with salt and leave for 30 minutes to dégorge. Rinse and drain well, then dry thoroughly with absorbent kitchen paper.

2. Combine the mushrooms with the cucumber, horseradish, lemon juice and yogurt. Fold in the trout, then add salt and pepper to taste.

3. Slice the tomatoes thickly, then sandwich in pairs with the trout mixture.

4. Arrange the tomato 'sandwiches' in a shallow serving dish. Garnish with spring onion and chill until ready to serve.

Smoked Cod Timbale

SERVES SIX

350 g (12 oz) long grain rice
15 ml (1 level tbsp) turmeric
7.5 ml (1½ level tsp) salt
350 g (12 oz) smoked cod fillet
1 small bunch spring onions, trimmed
2 eggs, hard-boiled
watercress sprigs and whole prawns, to garnish

Serve this attractive golden rice ring as a lunch, supper or buffet dish, accompanied by a side salad. Smoked haddock could be substituted if cod is not available.

1. Place the rice with the turmeric and salt in a saucepan of water and cook for 10–15 minutes. Drain well and cool.

2. Put the cod in a pan with a little water just to cover and poach for 12–15 minutes. Drain. Flake the fish, discarding the skin and bones.

3. Roughly chop the spring onions with the hard-boiled eggs. Mix with the cold rice and fish, adding salt and pepper to taste.

4. Spoon the mixture into an oiled 1.1 litre (2 pint) ring mould. Press down well, cover and chill for 2–3 hours.

5. To serve, unmould the fish ring on to a plate and garnish with watercress sprigs and prawns.

Marinated Kippers

SERVES FOUR

150 ml (¼ pint) olive oil
75 ml (5 tbsp) lemon juice
1.25 ml (¼ level tsp) mustard powder
1 small onion, skinned and very finely chopped
1–2 garlic cloves, skinned and crushed
4 boneless kipper fillets, skinned
a few raw onion rings, parsley sprigs and paprika, to garnish

Kippers are herrings which are split and gutted, soaked in brine, then smoked. The best are said to come from Loch Fyne in Scotland, although those from the Isle of Man are also considered to be very good. Serve this chilled starter with plenty of granary or home-made wholemeal bread.

1. In a jug, whisk together the oil, lemon juice, mustard, onion, garlic and pepper.

2. Put the kippers in a shallow dish and pour over the marinade. Cover and chill for at least 8 hours. Turn the kippers in the marinade occasionally during this time.

3. Remove the kippers from the marinade and cut each one in half lengthways. Fold each half over crossways, then place in a single layer in a dish.

4. Pour the marinade over the kippers and garnish the top with onion rings, parsley sprigs and a sprinkling of paprika.

Smoked Salmon Pâté

SERVES SIX

175 g (6 oz) smoked salmon 'off-cuts'
75 g (3 oz) unsalted butter, melted
20 ml (4 tsp) lemon juice
60 ml (4 tbsp) single cream
freshly ground pepper
cucumber slices, to garnish
150 ml (¼ pint) liquid aspic jelly

This elegant dinner party starter is easy to prepare and requires no cooking. Exquisitely flavoured smoked salmon is the most expensive smoked fish. This pâté uses 'off-cuts'—the cheaper small pieces left over when a whole side is cut up.

1. Roughly cut up the salmon pieces, reserving a few for garnishing, and place in a blender or food processor. Add the butter, lemon juice and cream, with freshly ground pepper to taste. Blend the mixture until smooth. Spoon into a 300 ml (½ pint) dish to within 1 cm (½ inch) of the rim. Chill for 1 hour to set.

2. Garnish with the reserved pieces of smoked salmon and cucumber slices. Spoon over the aspic jelly, which should be just on the point of setting. Refrigerate again for 30 minutes to set the aspic. Leave at room temperature for 30 minutes before serving.

Lettuce Dolmas with Smoked Mackerel Filling

SERVES SIX

1 large Cos lettuce
1 medium onion, skinned
50 g (2 oz) butter
45 ml (3 level tbsp) plain flour
150 ml ($\frac{1}{4}$ pint) milk
150 ml ($\frac{1}{4}$ pint) soured cream
salt and freshly ground pepper
30 ml (2 tbsp) lemon juice
100 g (4 oz) brown rice, cooked
2 hard-boiled eggs, chopped
225 g (8 oz) smoked mackerel fillet, skinned, boned and flaked
105 ml (7 tbsp) Fish Stock (see page 88)
herb butter, to garnish

To make a simple herb butter, combine 175 g (6 oz) butter with 60 ml (4 tbsp) chopped fresh parsley, 22.5 ml (1$\frac{1}{2}$ tbsp) snipped chives and 10 ml (2 tsp) lemon juice. Cover with foil and store in the refrigerator. Serve with the dolmas.

1. Ease off 12 lettuce leaves and cut out the tough stalk from the core end. Blanch a few at a time in a saucepan of boiling salted water for 1 minute. Drain.

2. Finely chop the onion with a further 4 medium-sized lettuce leaves. Melt the butter in a saucepan, add the chopped onion and lettuce and gently fry until softened.

3. Stir in the flour, milk, soured cream and salt and pepper to taste. Bring to the boil and simmer for 2 minutes, stirring. Add the lemon juice.

4. Stir the rice, egg and flaked mackerel into the sauce. Leave to cool. Adjust the seasoning.

5. Divide the filling into 12, wrap each portion in a blanched lettuce leaf. Pack in a single layer in an ovenproof dish; pour over the stock. Cover tightly.

6. Cook in the oven at 200°C (400°F) mark 6 for about 20 minutes. Top with herb butter for serving.

Smoked Salmon and Trout Mousses

SERVES SIX

450 g (1 lb) salmon trout, cleaned
300 ml ($\frac{1}{2}$ pint) milk
1 bay leaf and 6 peppercorns, to flavour
15 ml (3 level tsp) powdered gelatine
25 g (1 oz) butter
30 ml (2 level tbsp) plain flour
salt and freshly ground pepper
15 ml (1 tbsp) Dijon mustard
20 ml (4 tsp) tomato ketchup
175–225 g (6–8 oz) thinly sliced smoked salmon
150 ml ($\frac{1}{4}$ pint) double cream
150 ml ($\frac{1}{4}$ pint) Mayonnaise (see page 91)
30 ml (2 tbsp) lemon juice
black olives and lemon slices, to garnish

A special occasion first course to impress your guests. These mousses, coated in a thin layer of smoked salmon, are made from a rich, well-flavoured salmon and trout mixture.

1. Poach the trout in a saucepan in the milk with flavourings for about 20 minutes until tender. Drain, reserving the milk. Discard the head, skin and bones. Flake the flesh.

2. Place 45 ml (3 tbsp) very hot water in a bowl and sprinkle in the gelatine. Stir briskly.

3. Melt the butter in a saucepan, add the flour and cook gently, stirring, for 1–2 minutes. Remove from the heat and gradually blend in the reserved milk. Bring to the boil, stirring constantly, then simmer for 3 minutes until thick and smooth. Add salt and pepper to taste and stir in the soaked gelatine until dissolved.

4. In a blender or food processor, blend the sauce, fish, mustard and ketchup to form a smooth purée; cool.

5. Line six lightly oiled 175 ml (6 fl oz) ramekin dishes with the smoked salmon. Whip the cream until softly stiff. Stir the mayonnaise, lemon juice and cream into the fish mixture. Adjust the seasoning.

6. Spoon the mixture into the dishes, cover and refrigerate to set. Carefully turn out the mousses and garnish with black olives and lemon slices.

Smoked Mackerel with Apple

SERVES EIGHT

350 g (12 oz) smoked mackerel
100 g (4 oz) celery, trimmed and finely chopped
100 g (4 oz) cucumber, skinned and finely chopped
100 g (4 oz) red eating apples, cored and chopped
150 ml (¼ pint) soured cream
30 ml (2 tbsp) lemon juice
paprika pepper
1 small crisp lettuce, shredded

This healthy starter or lunch dish is best served with warm, crusty bread. Because of its high oil content, mackerel deteriorates quickly and that is why it is widely available preserved—smoked, pickled and salted.

1. Skin the mackerel, then flake the flesh roughly with a fork. Discard the bones.

2. Combine the celery, cucumber, apple and mackerel in a bowl. Stir in the soured cream, lemon juice and paprika to taste.

3. Place a little lettuce in the base of eight stemmed glasses. Divide the mackerel equally between them.

4. Garnish each glass with a lemon wedge, if liked, and sprinkle with paprika. Serve at room temperature.

Smoked Salmon and Cheese Tartlets

MAKES THIRTY TARTLETS

1–1½ quantities Shortcrust Pastry (see page 93)
175 g (6 oz) packet soft cheese with chopped chives
1 egg, beaten
150 ml (¼ pint) single cream
100 g (4 oz) smoked salmon 'off-cuts'
freshly ground pepper
about 50 g (2 oz) grated Parmesan
slices of radish and strips of canned pimiento and anchovy fillets, to garnish

These mouth-watering savoury tartlets are particularly good served with a selection of canapés for a buffet lunch or drinks party. The rich, creamy smoked salmon filling also includes two cheeses for added flavour—soft cheese with chives and Parmesan.

1. Roll out the pastry and cut 30 rounds each 6.5 cm (2½ inches). Put these in greased patty tins. Bake blind in the oven at 200°C (400°F) mark 6 for about 10 minutes.

2. Put the soft cheese in a bowl and

gradually beat in the egg and cream until the mixture is smooth.

3. Snip the smoked salmon in small pieces into the cheese mixture. Add pepper to taste.

4. Divide the filling equally between the tartlet cases and sprinkle with Parmesan cheese. Reduce the oven temperature to 180°C (350°F) mark 4 and bake for about 15 minutes or until the custard is set.

5. Transfer the tartlet cases to a wire rack and leave to cool for 30 minutes. Garnish.

Taramasalata

SERVES SIX

225 g (8 oz) smoked cod's roe
1 garlic clove, skinned and crushed
50 g (2 oz) fresh white breadcrumbs
1 small onion, skinned and finely chopped
grated rind and juice of 1 lemon
150 ml (¼ pint) olive oil

Taramasalata is a popular Greek dish eaten before a main meal. This creamy dip with a subtle flavour of smoked fish is easily made.

1. Skin the smoked cod's roe and break into pieces. Purée in a blender or food processor. Add the garlic, breadcrumbs, onion and lemon rind and juice to the cod's roe and blend for a few more seconds.

2. Gradually add the oil and blend well after each addition until smooth. Blend in 90 ml (6 tbsp) hot water with pepper to taste.

3. Spoon into a serving dish and chill for at least 1 hour. Garnish with lemon slices and serve with warmed pitta bread or toast, if liked.

Hot Mackerel Mousse

SERVES FOUR

450 g (1 lb) smoked mackerel fillets, skinned

15 ml (1 tbsp) white wine vinegar

salt and freshly ground pepper

25 g (1 oz) butter

25 g (1 oz) plain flour

300 ml (½ pint) milk

425 g (15 oz) can chick-peas, drained

150 ml (¼ pint) natural yogurt

3 eggs, separated

If you want to avoid those commercially produced smoked fish where synthetic flavourings and colourings are sometimes used, invest in a home-smoker. It takes little time—simply place the smoker in an open fireplace, to disperse the fumes, and leave until the metal container is cold.

1. Roughly flake the mackerel flesh. Beat in the vinegar and salt and pepper to taste.

2. Melt the butter in a saucepan, add the flour and cook gently, stirring, for 1–2 minutes. Remove from the heat and gradually blend in the milk. Bring to the boil, stirring constantly, then simmer for 3 minutes until thickened and smooth.

3. Purée the chick-peas, sauce, yogurt and egg yolks in a blender or food processor. Adjust seasoning.

4. Whisk the egg whites until they just hold their shape and fold into the chick-pea mixture.

5. Pour half into a well greased 2 litre (3½ pint) soufflé dish. Sprinkle the mackerel evenly on top and finish with remaining mixture.

6. Bake in the oven at 200°C (400°F) mark 6 for 45–50 minutes until well risen, golden and just set. Serve immediately.

Smoked Salmon Quiche

SERVES EIGHT TO TEN

225 g (8 oz) plain flour

salt and freshly ground pepper

115 g (4 oz) butter or margarine

1 egg yolk

10 ml (2 tsp) lemon juice

175 g (6 oz) full-fat soft cheese

300 ml (½ pint) single or double cream

3 eggs

175 g (6 oz) smoked salmon pieces

finely grated rind of 1 lemon

5 ml (1 level tsp) paprika

As this creamy quiche tastes equally good cold, it makes an excellent addition to a picnic or cold buffet spread.

1. Sift the flour and a pinch of salt together into a bowl. Cut the butter into small pieces and add to the flour. Rub in the butter with your fingertips until the mixture resembles fine breadcrumbs.

2. Add the egg yolk and half of the lemon juice, then add about 30 ml (2 tbsp) cold water to bind the mixture together in large lumps.

3. With one hand, collect the mixture together to form a ball. Knead lightly for a few seconds to give a firm, smooth dough. Do not overhandle.

4. Roll out the dough on a floured surface and use to line a 25.5 cm (10 inch) loose-bottomed metal flan tin. Chill for 30 minutes.

5. Prick the pastry base and then line with foil and fill with baking beans. Bake blind on a preheated baking sheet in the oven at 200°C (400°F) mark 6 for 10 minutes. Remove the foil and beans and return to the oven for a further 5 minutes. Reduce the oven temperature to 190°C (375°F) mark 5.

6. Prepare the filling. Put the cheese in a bowl and gradually whisk in the cream. When well mixed and smooth, add the eggs and beat well to mix.

7. Add the salmon, grated lemon rind and remaining lemon juice. Season with a little salt and plenty of pepper, then add half of the paprika and beat well to mix.

8. Pour the filling into the baked flan case and bake in the oven for 25–30 minutes until set. Sprinkle with the remaining paprika while very hot. Serve warm or cold.

BASIC RECIPES

Stocks & Sauces

*F*ish is such a versatile ingredient that it lends itself to a variety of treatments, both in cooking and serving. A selection of the most classic and tasty sauces is given on the following pages, as well as some of the basic bouillons and marinades frequently used in fish preparation. Recipes for the most commonly used pastry in fish cooking are also included.

RECIPES

Stocks, Bouillons & Marinades

FISH STOCK

Do not use bones or trimmings from oily fish such as salmon or trout.

Makes 1.1 litres (2 pints)

1 very small onion, skinned and chopped
3 parsley stalks
25 g (1 oz) mushroom trimmings
900 g (2 lb) fish bones and trimmings, such as sole, turbot, whiting
1.1 litres (2 pints) water
juice of $\frac{1}{4}$ lemon
5 ml (1 level tsp) salt
6 white peppercorns

1. Put the onion, parsley stalks and mushroom trimmings in a saucepan with the bones and fish trimmings. Cover with the water, lemon juice and add salt.

2. Bring to the boil, skim and simmer gently for 20 minutes.

3. Add the peppercorns and simmer for a further 10 minutes. Strain after 30 minutes to prevent the stock becoming cloudy. Use as required.

MARINADE FOR FISH

The time of marinating will depend on the thickness of the fish but 12 hours should be the maximum.

Makes 150 ml ($\frac{1}{4}$ pint)

150 ml ($\frac{1}{4}$ pint) olive oil
zest of $\frac{1}{2}$ lemon, cut into thin strips
1 thyme sprig
1 bay leaf
6 parsley stalks
1 basil sprig
$\frac{1}{2}$ small onion, skinned and thinly sliced
pinch of salt
pinch of fresh ground pepper

1. Mix all the ingredients in a container and leave for about 2 hours before adding the fish. Use as required.

PLAIN COURT BOUILLON

Use plain court bouillon for white fish such as brill or turbot. For whole fish, use the court bouillon cold and bring to the boil. For cuts of fish, place the fish into the hot court bouillon.

Makes 2.3 litres (4 pints)

$\frac{1}{2}$ lemon
2 litres (3$\frac{1}{2}$ pints) water
300 ml ($\frac{1}{2}$ pint) milk
25 g (1 oz) salt

1. Slice the lemon and remove pips. Put all ingredients in a large saucepan and bring to the boil. Use as required.

VINEGAR COURT BOUILLON

Use vinegar court bouillon for oily fish such as salmon or trout. For whole fish, use the court bouillon cold and bring to the boil. For cuts of fish, place the fish into the hot court bouillon.

Makes about 1.1 litres (2 pints)

1.1 litres (2 pints) water
100 ml (4 fl oz) vinegar
10 ml (2 tsp) coarse salt
100 g (4 oz) carrots, peeled and sliced
1 small onion, skinned and sliced
1 thyme sprig
1 bay leaf
2 parsley stalks
6 whole peppercorns

1. Place all ingredients except the peppercorns into a saucepan. Bring to the boil and simmer gently for 1 hour.

2. Add the peppercorns and simmer for a further 10 minutes. Strain and use as required.

Sauces & Butters

BÉARNAISE SAUCE

If preferred, the sauce can be cooked in a double saucepan, or in a heatproof bowl over a pan of gently simmering water.

Serves 4

1 shallot, skinned and finely chopped
20 ml (4 tsp) fresh tarragon, chopped
10 ml (2 tsp) fresh chervil, chopped
75 ml (3 fl oz) dry white wine
75 ml (3 fl oz) tarragon vinegar
pinch of crushed white peppercorns
pinch of salt
3 egg yolks
225 g (8 oz) butter, melted
freshly ground pepper

1. Put the shallot, 5 ml (1 tsp) of the tarragon, 2.5 ml (½ tsp) of the chervil, white wine and tarragon vinegar in a saucepan. Add the crushed peppercorns and salt and boil until reduced by two-thirds. Allow to cool.

2. Add the egg yolks and whisk over a gentle heat to form an emulsion.

3. Gradually add the warm melted butter, whisking well after each addition. Strain the sauce through muslin or a fine strainer.

4. Adjust the seasoning and stir in the remaining tarragon and chervil.

BÉCHAMEL SAUCE

This delicate white sauce is used as the base for classic Mornay sauce—(see page 90).

Makes 600 ml (1 pint)

40 g (1½ oz) butter
40 g (1½ oz) plain flour
568 ml (1 pint) milk
½ small onion, skinned and chopped
small thyme sprig
pinch of salt
pinch of freshly ground pepper
pinch of grated nutmeg

1. Melt the butter in a pan, add the flour and cook gently, stirring, for 1–2 minutes.

2. Remove from the heat and gradually blend in the milk. Bring to the boil and add the onion, thyme, salt, pepper and nutmeg to the sauce. Simmer gently for 10 minutes, stirring. Pass through a fine strainer.

BUTTER SAUCE (BEURRE BLANC)

This sauce is easy to prepare and is an ideal accompaniment for white fish dishes.

Serves 4

1 shallot, skinned and finely chopped
25 ml (1 fl oz) wine vinegar
225 g (8 oz) unsalted butter
7.5 ml (½ tbsp) lemon juice
pinch of salt
pinch of freshly ground pepper

1. Put the shallot, vinegar and 25 ml (1 fl oz) water into a saucepan. Bring to the boil and reduce by about two-thirds.

2. While boiling rapidly, add the butter and allow to melt.

3. Remove from the heat when emulsified and add the lemon juice, salt and pepper.

Variation

TARRAGON BUTTER SAUCE

Add 15 g (½ oz) chopped fresh tarragon to the prepared butter sauce.

FISH VELOUTÉ

Similar to Béchamel sauce, this uses fish stock instead of milk to produce a less creamy accompaniment.

Makes 600 ml (1 pint)

40 g (1½ oz) butter
40 g (1½ oz) plain flour
600 ml (1 pint) Fish Stock (see page 88)

1. Melt the butter in a saucepan, add the flour and cook gently, stirring, for 1–2 minutes.

2. Remove from the heat and gradually blend in the fish stock. Bring to the boil, stirring constantly, then simmer for 15 minutes. Use as required.

HOLLANDAISE SAUCE

Serve hollandaise lukewarm with poached salmon, salmon trout, sole, halibut or turbot.

Makes 600 ml (1 pint)

6 white peppercorns, crushed
25 ml (1 fl oz) wine vinegar
2 egg yolks
225 g (8 oz) unsalted butter, melted
pinch of salt
pinch of cayenne (optional)
juice of ¼ lemon

1. Put the peppercorns and vinegar in a saucepan and boil to reduce by two-thirds. Add 30 ml (2 tbsp) cold water. Cool.

2. Put the egg yolks and reduced vinegar liquid into a double saucepan or bowl over a pan of simmering water and whisk until the consistency of double cream is reached.

3. Remove from the heat and gradually add the warm melted butter, whisking well.

4. When all the butter is added, strain the sauce through muslin or a fine strainer. Add the salt and cayenne, if using, then stir in the lemon juice and a little hot water, if liked, to lighten the sauce.

MORNAY SAUCE

Makes 600 ml (1 pint)

1 quantity Béchamel Sauce (see page 89)
25 g (1 oz) Gruyère cheese, grated
25 g (1 oz) Parmesan cheese, grated
25 g (1 oz) butter

1. Heat the béchamel sauce in a saucepan. Stir in the Gruyère and Parmesan. Reheat for a few seconds, then swirl in the butter.

TARTARE SAUCE

The classic sauce for fried fish.

Serves 4

1 quantity Mayonnaise (see page 91)
25 g (1 oz) capers, finely chopped
50 g (2 oz) gherkins, finely chopped
15 g (½ oz) chopped fresh parsley

1. Mix the mayonnaise with the capers, gherkins and parsley in a bowl. Adjust the consistency and seasoning if necessary.

TOMATO SAUCE

A fresh-tasting alternative to the more common rich cream sauces.

Makes 600 ml (1 pint)

450 g (1 lb) tomatoes, skinned
25 ml (1 fl oz) olive oil
1 small shallot, skinned and chopped
1 small garlic clove, skinned and crushed
15 g (½ oz) tomato purée
300 ml (½ pint) Fish Stock (see page 88)
1 bouquet garni
pinch of salt
pinch of freshly ground pepper
7.5 ml (½ level tbsp) sugar

1. Cut the tomatoes in half and press to remove the seeds and excess moisture. Heat the oil in a saucepan, add the shallot and garlic and cook gently without colouring.

2. Add the tomatoes, tomato purée, fish stock and bouquet garni. Add salt, pepper and sugar, cover and simmer for 20 minutes.

3. Remove the bouquet garni. Purée the sauce in a blender, or press through a sieve. If too thin, return to the pan and boil to reduce.

SAUCE DUXELLES

A tasty brown mushroom sauce, ideal for firm-fleshed white fish.

Makes about 600 ml (1 pint)

5 ml (1 tsp) butter
5 ml (1 tsp) vegetable oil
1 small shallot, skinned and finely chopped
150 g (5 oz) mushrooms, wiped and finely chopped
pinch of salt
pinch of freshly ground pepper
30 ml (2 tbsp) chopped fresh parsley
175 ml (6 fl oz) dry white wine
15 ml (1 tbsp) tomato purée
300 ml (½ pint) Fish Velouté (see page 89)

1. To make the duxelles, heat the butter and oil in a pan and gently fry half the shallot without colouring. Add the mushrooms and cook gently until the moisture has evaporated. Sprinkle with salt and pepper and add a little of the chopped parsley.

2. To make the sauce, put the white wine with the remaining shallot in a pan and boil until reduced by two-thirds. Add the tomato purée, fish velouté and duxelles and simmer gently for 5 minutes. Stir in the remaining chopped parsley.

GARLIC BUTTER

Makes 225 g (8 oz)

1 garlic clove, skinned and crushed
225 g (8 oz) unsalted butter, softened
5 ml (1 tsp) lemon juice
freshly ground pepper
30 ml (2 tbsp) chopped fresh parsley

1. Mash the garlic into the butter in a bowl. Mix in the lemon juice, pepper and chopped parsley. Leave for a few hours before use.

CLARIFIED BUTTER

Makes 225 g (8 oz)

225 g (8 oz) unsalted butter

1. Melt the butter gently in a heavy-based saucepan. Simmer until a thick froth appears.

2. Continue to simmer the butter for 10–20 minutes until the froth starts to separate from the clear golden liquid, and some of the sediment settles at the bottom. Keep checking the butter as it burns easily.

3. Remove from the heat and cool slightly. Line a sieve with muslin or absorbent kitchen paper. Place over a bowl and carefully pour the butter through the sieve, taking care not to disturb the sediment.

4. Leave to cool slightly, then transfer to a jar, cover and refrigerate for up to 3–4 weeks.

Mayonnaise
CLASSIC MAYONNAISE

When making mayonnaise, have all the ingredients at the same temperature to avoid separation during the mixing process. The ingredients must not be too cold. Lemon juice produces a whiter mayonnaise. A variety of oils can be used for mayonnaise: olive oil is the finest but very expensive, corn oil produces a good quality mayonnaise with little real flavour.

Serves 4

2 egg yolks
7.5 ml ($\frac{1}{2}$ tbsp) wine vinegar or juice of $\frac{1}{4}$–$\frac{1}{2}$ lemon
pinch of salt
pinch of ground white pepper
300 ml ($\frac{1}{2}$ pint) vegetable oil

1. Mix the egg yolks and vinegar or lemon juice with the salt and pepper in a bowl. Whisk well.

2. Gradually add the oil, a little at a time, making sure that each addition is incorporated before adding more.

3. When all the oil is mixed in, adjust the seasoning, then add 15 ml (1 tbsp) boiling water, which will stabilise the sauce and give it a glossy appearance.

Variation
DILL MAYONNAISE

If using dill pickle, thin the mayonnaise slightly with a little of the preserving liquid.

Serves 4

1 quantity Mayonnaise
15 g ($\frac{1}{2}$ oz) finely chopped fresh dill or dill pickle

1. Mix the mayonnaise with the dill in a bowl.

Variation
GARLIC MAYONNAISE

Serves 4

1 quantity Mayonnaise
1 garlic clove, skinned and crushed

1. Mix the mayonnaise with the crushed garlic in a bowl. Leave for 2 hours for the garlic to permeate the mayonnaise. Adjust the seasoning if necessary.

Variation
HORSERADISH MAYONNAISE

Serves 4

1 quantity Mayonnaise
25 ml (1 fl oz) horseradish sauce

1. Mix the mayonnaise with the horseradish sauce in a bowl. Add a little water to thin to coating consistency.

Pastry
PUFF PASTRY

Makes 900 g (2 lb)

450 g (1 lb) strong plain flour
pinch of salt
450 g (1 lb) butter
about 300 ml (½ pint) cold water
15 ml (1 tbsp) lemon juice
beaten egg, to glaze

1. Mix the flour and a pinch of salt together in a large mixing bowl.

2. Cut off 50 g (2 oz) butter and pat the remaining butter with a rolling pin to a square slab 2 cm (¾ inch) thick.

3. Rub the 50 g (2 oz) butter into the flour with the finger and thumb tips. Stir in enough water and lemon juice to make a soft, elastic dough.

4. Knead dough until smooth and shape into a square. Roll out to make a square 20 × 20 cm (8 × 8 inches).

5. Place the slab of butter to form a diamond in the centre of the dough and fold over the flaps, envelope-style. Press gently with a rolling pin.

6. Roll out into a rectangle measuring about 40 × 20 cm (16 × 8 inches). Fold the bottom third up and the top third down, keeping the edges straight. Seal the edges by pressing with the rolling pin.

7. Wrap the pastry in greaseproof paper and leave in the refrigerator to rest for 30 minutes.

8. Put the pastry on a lightly floured

working surface with the folded edges to the sides and repeat the rolling, folding and resting sequence five times.

9. After the final resting, roll out the pastry on a lightly floured surface and shape as required. Brush with beaten egg. The usual oven temperature is 230°C (450°F) mark 8.

ROUGH PUFF PASTRY

Makes 400 g (14 oz)

225 g (8 oz) plain flour
pinch of salt
75 g (3 oz) butter or block margarine
75 g (3 oz) lard
about 150 ml (¼ pint) cold water
a squeeze of lemon juice
beaten egg, to glaze

1. Mix the flour and salt together in a bowl. Cut the butter and lard (which should be quite firm) into cubes about 2 cm (¾ inch) across.

2. Stir the fat into the flour without breaking up the pieces. Add enough water and lemon juice to mix to a fairly stiff dough.

3. On a lightly floured surface, roll out into an oblong three times as long as it is wide. Fold the bottom third up and the top third down, then turn the pastry so that the folded edges are at the sides. Seal the ends of the pastry by pressing lightly with a rolling pin.

4. Repeat this rolling and folding process three more times, turning the dough so that the folded edge is on the left hand side each time.

5. Wrap the pastry in greaseproof paper and leave to rest in the refrigerator or a cool place for about 30 minutes before using.

6. Roll out the pastry on a lightly floured surface to 3 mm (1/8 inch) thick and use as required. Brush with beaten egg before baking. The usual oven temperature is 220°C (425°F) mark 7.

FLAKY PASTRY

Makes 400 g (14 oz)

225 g (8 oz) plain flour
pinch of salt
75 g (3 oz) butter or block margarine
75 g (3 oz) lard
about 150 ml (¼ pint) cold water
a squeeze of lemon juice
beaten egg, to glaze

1. Mix the flour and salt together in a bowl. Soften the butter and lard by working them together with a knife on a plate, divide it into four equal portions.

2. Add one quarter of the fat to the flour and rub it in between finger and thumb tips until the mixture resembles fine breadcrumbs.

3. Add enough water and lemon juice to make a soft elastic dough, stirring it in with a round-bladed knife.

4. Turn the dough on to a lightly floured surface and roll out in to an oblong three times as long as it is wide.

5. Using a round-bladed knife, dot another quarter of the fat over the top two-thirds of the pastry in flakes, so that it looks like buttons on a card.

6. Fold the bottom third of the pastry up and the top third down and turn it so that the folded edges are at the side. Seal the edges of the pastry by pressing with a rolling pin.

7. Re-roll as before and repeat the process twice more until the remaining portions of fat have been used up.

8. Wrap the pastry loosely in greaseproof paper and leave it to rest in the refrigerator or a cool place for at least 30 minutes before using.

9. Roll out the pastry on a lightly floured working surface to 3 mm (1/8 inch) thick and use as required. Brush with beaten egg before baking to give the characteristic glaze. When cooking flaky pastry, the usual oven temperature is 220°C (425°F) mark 7.

SHORTCRUST PASTRY

When a recipe requires 175 g (6 oz) pastry, this refers to the weight of flour. For any quantity of shortcrust pastry, always use half fat to flour.

175 g (6 oz) plain flour
pinch of salt
75 g (3 oz) butter or block margarine and lard
about 30 ml (2 tbsp) cold water

1. Mix the flour and salt together in a bowl. Cut the butter into small pieces and add it to the flour.

2. Using both hands, rub the fat into the flour between finger and thumb tips until the mixture resembles fine breadcrumbs.

3. Add the water, sprinkling it evenly over the surface. Stir it in with a round-bladed knife until the mixture begins to stick together in large lumps.

4. With one hand, collect the mixture together and knead lightly for a few seconds to give a firm, smooth dough. The pastry can be used straight away, but is better allowed to rest for about 30 minutes. It can also be wrapped in cling film and kept in the refrigerator for a day or two.

5. Sprinkle a very little flour on a working surface and the rolling pin, not on the pastry, and roll out the dough evenly in one direction only, turning it occasionally. The ideal thickness is usually about 3 mm (1/8 inch). Do not pull or stretch the pastry. When cooking shortcrust pastry, the usual oven temperature is 200–220°C (400–425°F) mark 6–7.

TECHNIQUES

Some cooks are put off buying and cooking fish because they are unsure how to prepare it. On the following pages, clear step-by-step instructions are provided for the most commonly available fish, so that even the most inexperienced cook will be able to produce fish dishes with confidence.

Choosing Fish

Most fish have seasons when they are either available in large quantities or are considered at their best, so refer to the chart on pages 103–105 to know when to buy the best fish at a good price.

All fish should have only a mild, seaweedy smell; if there is the slightest whiff of ammonia, or even a 'fishy' smell, do not buy. When looking for really fresh, good-quality fish, appearance as well as smell will tell you whether it is in good condition. Whole fish should have shiny, protruding eyes with clear black centres, bright red gills, fresh colour, glistening scales and some natural slime. The flesh should be firm, not soft and floppy. Fresh fillets and steaks should look freshly cut, with moist, firm-textured flesh. Do not purchase fish which appears dry or discoloured. Avoid any fish with sunken, cloudy eyes and faded pink or grey gills.

Shellfish should be eaten absolutely fresh as it deteriorates faster than fish, so buy from a reliable source and cook and eat it the same day. It should have no smell.

When choosing smoked fish, the surface should be bright, glossy and clean. The flesh should be firm and springy to the touch, with a pleasant, smokey smell.

Storing Fish

FRESH FISH

If possible, buy fish on the day it is to be eaten. Keep the fish in a cool place until it can be put in the upper part of the refrigerator. Fish can be stored for up to 24 hours, if it is loosely wrapped in cling film or foil.

FROZEN FISH

Fish must be frozen within 24 hours of being caught. Most commercially frozen fish is of high quality—freezing does not affect the flavour or food value. When buying frozen fish, keep chilled in an insulated bag, or wrapped in newspaper, until it can be placed in its original wrappings in the freezing compartment of the refrigerator or in the freezer. It must not be allowed to defrost. The recommended storage time is usually marked on commercially frozen fish. As a rule of thumb, white fish will keep for about 3 months and oily fish for about 2 months. After this, the flavour deteriorates. Cooked fish dishes should not be kept longer than 2 months. Do not freeze your own shellfish as the temperature required will not be low enough.

THAWING FISH

Usually fish can be cooked from frozen. This is especially so with fish coated in batter or egg and breadcrumbs, which must be cooked from frozen for best results. However, larger fish such as salmon should be thawed thoroughly before cooking. Thaw fish in the refrigerator, drain and pat dry with absorbent kitchen paper. It should never be refrozen.

Preparing Fish

SCALING FISH

Soak the fish for a few minutes in cold water to facilitate scaling. Lay the fish on a work surface or wooden board covered with newspaper.

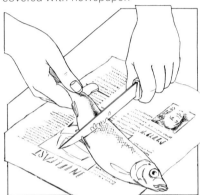

Grip the fish firmly at the tail end and scrape off the scales with the back of a firm-bladed knife, holding it almost at right angles to the body of the fish and working from the tail end to the head. Turn the fish over and remove the scales from the other side. Frequently rinse the fish under cold running water during and after scaling to remove the loose scales.

CLEANING FISH

The method of cleaning will be determined by the fish shape. In round fish, the entrails lie in the belly, whereas in flat fish they are found in a cavity behind the head. Wash sea fish under cold running water, soak freshwater fish in several changes of cold salt water until no muddy water remains.

Cleaning Round Fish

Using a sharp knife, slit open the soft belly from behind the gills to just above the tail.

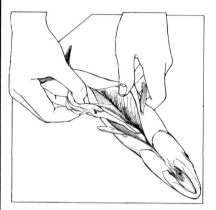

Holding the fish firmly in one hand, scrape out and discard the entrails. Open out the fish and rinse it under cold running water. If there is a line of blood or black skin along the spine, gently rub it away using a little salt.

If the fish is to be served whole, cut off the fins and gills. The head and tail may also be cut off, if you prefer.

To remove the head and tail, cut the head off with a sharp knife just below the gills.

To remove the head of a large fish with a strong backbone, cut down to the bone on both sides of the head. Bend back the head until the bone snaps: cut through the flesh to remove the head.

To remove a dorsal fin, make a deep incision on either side of it using a sharp knife. Pull the fin out firmly to bring the root bones with it.

Cleaning Flat Fish

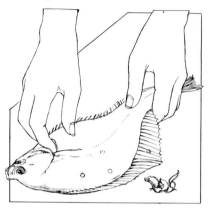

Make a semi-circular slit just below the gills by the head on the dark-skinned side. Pull or squeeze out the entrails and rinse the fish under cold running water. Cut off the fins with a sharp knife.

If serving whole, you may prefer to cut diagonally across the head to remove the eyes and mouth.

SKINNING FISH

Flat fish are often skinned before cooking, whereas round fish are usually left intact unless they are being cooked as fillets.

Skinning an Uncooked Round Fish

Cut off a narrow strip of skin along the backbone of the fish with a sharp knife. Loosen the skin just below and under the head, then gently pull it down towards the tail, working carefully to avoid breaking the flesh. Cut off the loose skin, then skin the other side of the fish in the same way.

Skinning an Uncooked Flat Fish

Cut off the fins. Lay the fish, dark skin uppermost, on a board. Make an incision across the skin of the fish, just above the tail.

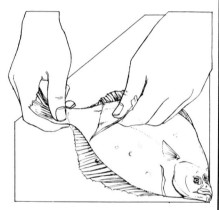

Slip the thumb into the slit and gently loosen the dark skin. Holding the fish firmly with one hand by the tail, pull the skin quickly upwards towards the head (if necessary, dip the fingers in a little salt to get a better grip). Cut the skin off. The white skin on the other side may be removed, but is generally left on.

Skinning a Fillet

Lay the fillet, skin side down and, with the tip of the knife, loosen enough skin at the tail end to give a good hold. Salt the fingers and, holding the loosened skin down with one hand, cut the flesh free from the skin with a sharp knife using a sawing action.

FILLETING AND BONING

After cleaning, the fish can be filleted into serving portions. A round fish will yield two fillets; a flat fish will yield four fillets, two from each side. The same basic techniques can be used to bone cooked fish.

Filleting Round Fish

To fillet a large, cleaned fish, such as haddock, first cut off the head. Cut along the backbone from tail to head, cutting to the bone.

Then working from the head to the tail, gently ease the fillet cleanly from the bones, using short, sharp, slicing strokes. Cut off the fillet at the tail.

Using the knife, ease off the backbone to reveal the second fillet. Cut off the tail. If the fish is large, the fillets may be halved. Skin if preferred.

Filleting Flat Fish

Cut off the fins. Then make a cut down the backbone through the flesh, working from the head to the tail.

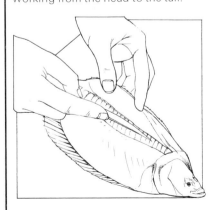

Make a semi-circular cut just below the head.

Then, slanting the knife against the backbone, separate the left fillet using long, angled strokes to the bone. Cut just above the tail to remove the fillet.

Turn the fish around and work from the tail towards the head to free the second right hand fillet. Turn the fish over and remove the other two fillets in the same way.

Boning a Large Cooked Round Fish

Place the cooked salmon or sea trout on a board and, using a sharp knife, snip the skin just below the head and above the tail. Carefully peel off the skin, working from the head to the tail.

Snip the backbone below the head and above the tail. Then, with a sharp knife, split the fish along the backbone. Gently lift out the backbone without breaking the fish in two.

Boning a Small Round Fish

Smaller round fish, such as mackerel and trout, can be filleted but are often boned and cooked whole.

Clean the fish first, then cut off the head, tail and fins if necessary. Open out the fish and spread it flat on a board, skin side up.

Run a thumb firmly down the centre back of the fish to loosen the backbone.

Turn the fish over and ease away the backbone with the tip of a knife or the fingers, working from the head end. Remove as many small bones as possible at the same time. Either fold back the fish to its original shape, or cut into two fillets.

Preparing Molluscs and Shellfish

PREPARING AND COOKING COCKLES

Cockles are usually sold cooked, with or without their shells. To prepare fresh cockles, immerse the tightly closed shells in a bucket of salted water for about 1 hour to remove the sand. Scrub the shells under cold running water. Place in a saucepan containing 1 cm ($\frac{1}{2}$ inch) water, cover and boil for about 5 minutes until the shells open, shaking the pan regularly. Drain.

PREPARING AND COOKING MUSSELS

Mussels must always be bought alive and completely fresh. Discard any with broken shells or ones that do not close when tapped. Steep the closed mussels in a sink full of cold salted water and leave them to soak for 1 hour or more. Throw away any mussels that float. Clean the soaked mussels by scrubbing with a stiff brush to remove all grit.

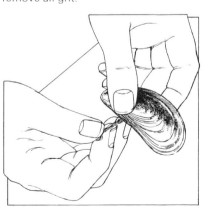

Using a sharp knife, scrape off any barnacles growing on the shells and pull off the beards (the seaweed-like strands protruding from each shell). The final washing water should be clean.

To cook mussels, put 1 cm ($\frac{1}{2}$ inch) water in a large saucepan and add the drained, cleaned mussels. Bring to the boil, cover and steam for about 5 minutes until the shells open, shaking the pan occasionally. Remove the mussels from the pan, discarding any that remain closed. Use as required.

PREPARING OYSTERS

Oysters are sold live in the shell, and may be eaten raw in their half shell, served on a bed of cracked ice, or cooked.

Scrub the tightly closed oysters with a stiff brush under cold running water to remove all sand. Discard any that are open or remain open when tapped.

To open oysters, an oyster knife, with its thick handle and short cone-

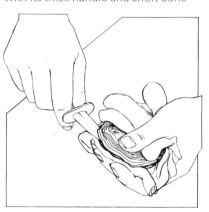

shaped blade, is essential. However, any knife with a short, strong blade may be used.

As oyster shells are rough, you may prefer to hold them with a cloth. Place the shell on the palm with the flattest side uppermost. Insert the tip of the knife into the hinge linking the shells and cut through the ligament. Push the blade in between the shells and cut round the hinge. Prise the shells apart, twisting the knife firmly. Discard the top shell. Clean out any bits of broken shell with the knife. Scrape off the beard and cut away the oyster. Be careful not to spill the liquid.

PREPARING CLAMS

Clams, whether hard- or soft-shelled, are sold live in the shell, and can be eaten raw or cooked. To open clams, first scrub the shells under cold running water to remove the sand. Soft-shelled clams are easily opened by inserting a sharp knife. Hard-shelled clams need to be prised open with a knife and the muscle forming the hinge severed. Discard the top shell. To remove the clam, cut between the clam and the shell.

Cook clams as mussels (see far left), discarding any that remain closed when cooked.

PREPARING SCALLOPS

If buying scallops in the shell, select those with tightly closed shells. If you wish to use the pretty fan-shaped shells, scrub, then sterilise in boiling water first.

To prepare, hold the scallop in a cloth, with the flat shell uppermost. Insert a small knife into one of the openings on either side of the shell and run the blade along to one side to sever the muscle attaching the meat to the shell.

Pull the shells apart. Slide the knife under the grey outer rim of flesh, called the skirt, to free the scallop. Remove the white muscle and coral, then discard the remainder.

PREPARING A CRAB

Crabs are usually sold already cooked. If using the shell for dressed crab, first wash and dry it.

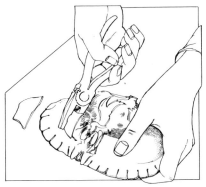

Then, using pincers or pliers, remove the thin undershell, following the natural line. Rub the shell with a little oil to give it gloss.

Lay the crab on its back and, holding it firmly by the shell, twist off the claws and legs. Set these aside.

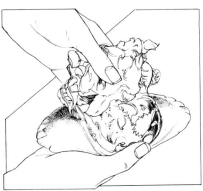

With the tail flap towards you, hold the shell firmly and push the body section up and out of the shell, using the thumbs. Discard the small stomach sac behind the crab's mouth.

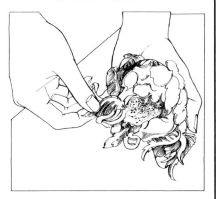

Pull away the grey gills, called dead men's fingers, that are attached to the body, and discard them. Cut the body section into four, remove the white flesh with a skewer, and place in a bowl. Using a small spoon, scoop out the brown meat from inside the shell, and place in a separate bowl to that of the white meat.

Crack the claws with a lobster cracker, small hammer or rolling pin and remove the white meat. Work the white meat from the leg sockets.

PREPARING LOBSTER

Although often sold ready-boiled, to enjoy a lobster at its best, it should be bought live.

If the lobster is to be used in a recipe which calls for an uncooked lobster, kill it first.

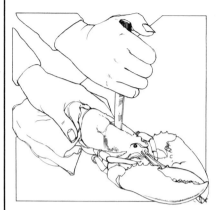

To do this, cover the tail with a cloth and, holding it firmly, plunge the point of a sharp knife into the place where the head meets the body, thus severing the spinal cord. (You may prefer to do this anyway before boiling the lobster.)

To boil a lobster, first tie the large claws with rubber bands. Place in a saucepan filled with cold salted water. Bring slowly to the boil, cover and simmer for 15–25 minutes until the shell is bright red. Leave to cool in the water. (Lobsters lose consciousness at 21°C (70°F) and die painlessly at 30°C (85°F).) However, lobster can be cooked by placing it directly into boiling salted water or court bouillon.

To remove the lobster meat, you need a lobster pick or shell cracker, if you don't have these, a spoon and hammer will suffice. Break the claws and legs off the lobster by twisting them at the joint. Crack the large claws with a shell cracker or hammer and remove the meat. Use a skewer to remove the meat from the legs. To extract the meat from the body and tail, lay the lobster on its back.

Cut down each side with a knife. Pull away the bony underside. Prise the flesh free, starting at the tail end. Discard the dark vein. Reserve the red roe or coral to garnish or add to lobster butter or sauce. The khaki-coloured liver or tomalley can also be eaten or added to a sauce. Using a lobster pick, point of a knife or spoon, pick the meat out of the head. Discard the stomach sac and greyish gills.

PREPARING PRAWNS

Hold the prawn in your left hand just behind the head. Gently break off the head and shell. Twist and pull away the tail shell. Turn the prawn over and peel off the main body shell in one piece, complete with legs. If there is any roe present, remove it by rinsing the prawn under cold running water.

PREPARING DUBLIN BAY PRAWNS

Using scissors, cut off the head. Push the sharp point of the scissors under

the shell along the curved back to the tail. Press back the shell at the head end with your fingers and gently ease out the prawn. Holding the end of the tail, pull the tail free of the shell.

PREPARING SQUID

The edible parts of a squid are the body pouch and fins, and the tentacles.

To prepare the squid, first wash it thoroughly in cold water.

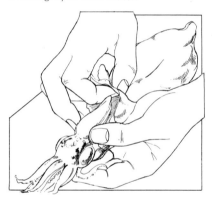

Draw back the rim of the body pouch, grasp the quill-shaped pen, gently pull it out and discard.

Grip the head and tentacles and pull the two sections gently apart. Cut the tentacles off the head, then discard the head, entrails, suckers, horny, beak-like mouth and ink sac. (If the ink sac is required, make sure it remains intact.)

Slip a finger under the skin on the body pouch and pull away. Skin the fins.

Cooking Fish

One of the great advantages of fish is that a nutritious main meal can be prepared in hardly any time at all. Fish can be grilled, steamed, poached, baked, shallow- and deep-fried or cooked in foil in the oven—a conveniently clean and odour-free cooking method.

The flesh of fish changes from translucent to opaque white or pink when cooked and it will flake easily when tested with a fork and come away cleanly from the bone. Never overcook fish as both texture and flavour will be spoilt.

GRILLING

A fast and simple cooking method, producing well-flavoured results. Preheat the grill to moderate, grease the grill rack or cover it with foil, if preferred. Brush oil or melted butter over white fish to prevent it from drying out during cooking—oily fish does not usually require this.

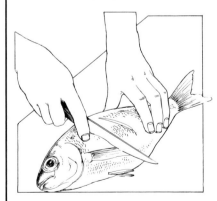

Make about three diagonal scores using a sharp knife on whole fish, such

as mackerel or herring, to allow the heat to penetrate. Thin fillets or steaks require grilling on one side only; thicker pieces and whole fish should be turned once. Allow 4–5 minutes for thin fillets, and 10–15 minutes for thicker pieces.

STEAMING

A gentle cooking method for a few thin fillets or slices, particularly sole or plaice. Place the fish on a greased, heatproof plate. Dot with butter, add a little milk with salt and pepper. Cover with foil and place over a saucepan of simmering water. Cook for about 10–15 minutes.

POACHING

In this method, fish is very gently simmered in a pan on top of the cooker or in a covered dish in the oven, usually in a court bouillon (see page 88), the liquid should cover the fish completely. Almost any fish is suitable, from fillets to a whole salmon. Allow 10–15 minutes per 450 g (1 lb) or 5–10 minutes for steaks. If the fish is to be served cold, leave to cool in the poaching liquid. This liquid may be strained and used in a sauce to serve with the fish.

BAKING

Whole fish, fillets or steaks can be baked in the oven at 180°C (350°F) mark 4. It is an ideal cooking method for stuffed fish. The fish is moistened with a little fish stock, milk or butter, then usually covered with buttered foil or a lid and baked until tender. Allow

10–12 minutes for fillets, 20 minutes for steaks and 25–30 minutes for small whole fish. A larger stuffed fish will take up to 1 hour.

SHALLOW FRYING

A suitable method for fillets, steaks and small, whole fish. First coat the fish in seasoned flour or beaten egg and breadcrumbs. Then heat enough oil, butter or a mixture of the two in a frying pan to a depth of 3 mm ($\frac{1}{8}$ inch). When hot, fry the fish until golden brown then turn over and cook the other side. Drain on absorbent kitchen paper. Allow about 10 minutes frying time, depending on the thickness of the fish.

DEEP FRYING

Most fish, except really thick pieces, and some shellfish such as scallops, mussels and prawns can be coated in egg and breadcrumbs or batter and deep fried. Oil or lard may be used; this can be used several times but should be kept for fish frying only. Heat the oil or fat to 177–188°C (350–370°F) using a thermometer. Alternatively, drop a 2.5 cm (1 inch) cube of bread into the oil or fat; it should turn golden in 1 minute. The pan should be no more than half full. For coated fish, use a wire basket. For battered fish, do not use the wire basket as the batter tends to stick to it; instead use tongs or a fish slice to put the fish into the fat and a perforated spoon to remove it.

Cook the fish for 5–10 minutes, depending on size, until golden brown. Drain well on absorbent kitchen paper.

FISH GUIDE

*T*he charts on the following pages provide an at-a-glance guide, both to the availability of fresh fish, and to the various cooking methods that can be used to prepare them.

FISH SEASONAL CHART

Round White Fish

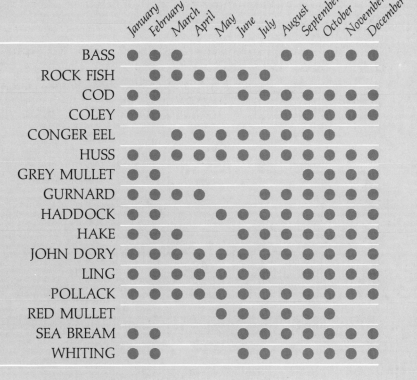

	January	February	March	April	May	June	July	August	September	October	November	December
BASS	●	●	●					●	●	●	●	●
ROCK FISH		●	●	●	●	●	●					
COD	●	●					●	●	●	●	●	●
COLEY	●	●						●	●	●	●	●
CONGER EEL			●	●	●	●	●	●	●	●	●	●
HUSS	●	●						●	●	●	●	●
GREY MULLET	●							●	●	●	●	●
GURNARD	●	●	●	●				●	●	●	●	●
HADDOCK	●	●			●	●	●	●	●	●	●	●
HAKE	●	●				●	●	●	●	●	●	●
JOHN DORY	●	●	●	●	●	●	●		●	●	●	●
LING	●	●	●	●	●	●			●	●	●	●
POLLACK	●	●	●	●	●	●			●	●	●	●
RED MULLET				●	●	●	●	●	●			
SEA BREAM	●	●					●	●	●	●	●	●
WHITING	●	●						●	●	●	●	●

Most fish are available throughout the year, although the months when they are at their best vary according to their spawning season. However, the seasons for fish vary around the country and supplies may also be affected by bad weather conditions.

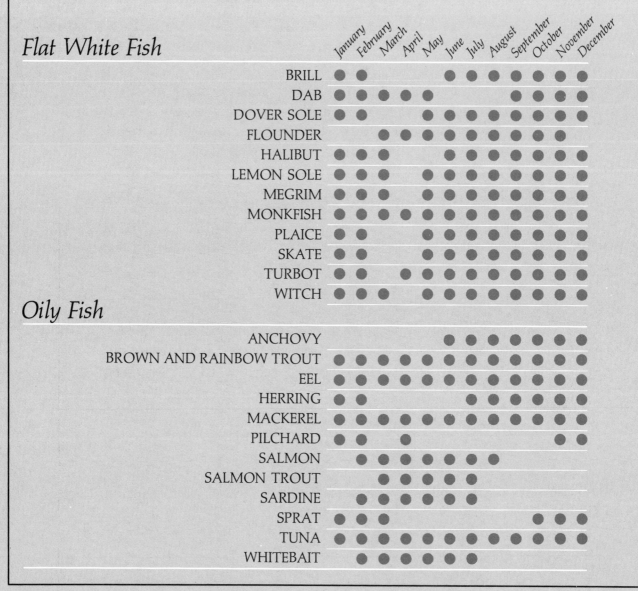

Flat White Fish

	Jan	Feb	Mar	Apr	May	Jun	Jul	Aug	Sep	Oct	Nov	Dec
BRILL	●	●				●	●	●	●	●	●	●
DAB	●	●	●	●	●				●	●	●	●
DOVER SOLE	●	●			●	●	●	●	●	●	●	●
FLOUNDER			●	●	●			●	●	●	●	●
HALIBUT	●	●	●			●	●	●	●	●	●	●
LEMON SOLE	●	●	●	●	●	●	●	●	●	●	●	●
MEGRIM	●	●	●	●	●	●	●	●	●	●	●	●
MONKFISH	●	●	●	●	●	●	●	●	●	●	●	●
PLAICE	●	●			●	●	●	●	●	●	●	●
SKATE	●	●			●	●	●	●	●	●	●	●
TURBOT	●	●			●	●	●	●	●	●	●	●
WITCH	●	●	●		●	●	●	●	●	●	●	●

Oily Fish

	Jan	Feb	Mar	Apr	May	Jun	Jul	Aug	Sep	Oct	Nov	Dec
ANCHOVY						●	●	●	●	●	●	●
BROWN AND RAINBOW TROUT	●	●	●	●	●	●	●	●	●	●	●	●
EEL	●	●	●	●	●	●	●	●	●	●	●	●
HERRING	●	●						●	●	●	●	●
MACKEREL	●	●	●	●	●	●	●	●	●	●	●	●
PILCHARD	●	●		●							●	●
SALMON			●	●	●	●	●	●				
SALMON TROUT				●	●	●	●					
SARDINE		●	●	●	●	●	●					
SPRAT	●	●	●							●	●	●
TUNA	●	●	●	●	●	●	●	●	●	●	●	●
WHITEBAIT		●	●	●	●	●						

Shellfish

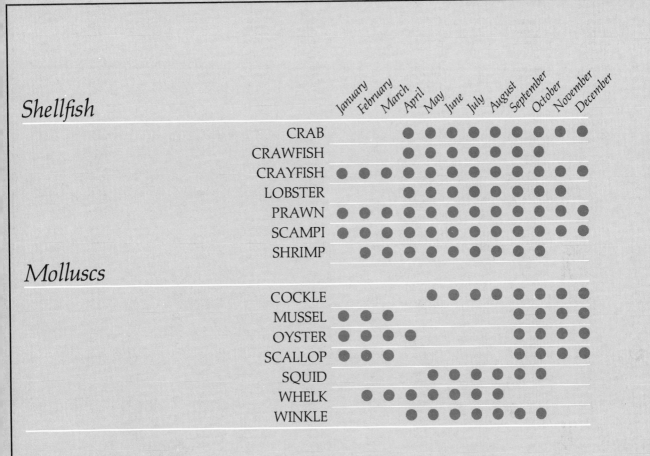

Molluscs

FISH COOKING CHART

Round White Fish

	Boiling/Poaching	Steaming	Baking	Shallow frying	Deep frying	Grilling
BASS	●	●	●	●		●
ROCK FISH	●	●	●	●	●	●
COD	●	●	●	●	●	●
COLEY	●	●	●	●		
CONGER EEL	●		●	●		
HUSS	●		●	●		
GREY MULLET		●		●		●
GURNARD			●	●		
HADDOCK	●	●	●	●	●	●
HAKE	●	●	●	●	●	●
JOHN DORY	●	●	●	●	●	
LING	●		●	●		
POLLACK	●	●	●	●		
RED MULLET			●	●		●
SEA BREAM	●		●	●		●
WHITING	●	●	●	●	●	●

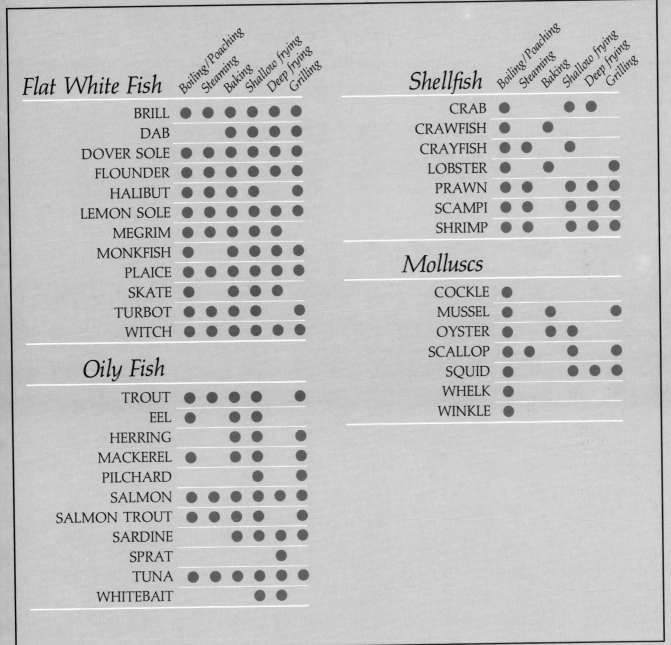

Flat White Fish

	Boiling/Poaching	Steaming	Baking	Shallow frying	Deep frying	Grilling
BRILL	●	●	●	●	●	●
DAB		●	●	●	●	
DOVER SOLE	●	●	●	●	●	●
FLOUNDER	●	●	●	●	●	●
HALIBUT	●	●	●	●	●	●
LEMON SOLE	●	●	●	●	●	●
MEGRIM	●	●	●	●		
MONKFISH	●		●	●		●
PLAICE	●	●	●	●	●	●
SKATE	●		●	●	●	
TURBOT	●	●	●	●		●
WITCH	●	●	●	●	●	

Oily Fish

	Boiling/Poaching	Steaming	Baking	Shallow frying	Deep frying	Grilling
TROUT	●	●	●	●		●
EEL	●		●	●		
HERRING			●	●		●
MACKEREL	●		●	●		●
PILCHARD				●		●
SALMON	●	●	●	●		●
SALMON TROUT	●	●	●	●		●
SARDINE			●	●	●	●
SPRAT				●		
TUNA	●	●	●	●	●	●
WHITEBAIT				●	●	

Shellfish

	Boiling/Poaching	Steaming	Baking	Shallow frying	Deep frying	Grilling
CRAB	●			●	●	
CRAWFISH	●		●			
CRAYFISH	●	●		●		
LOBSTER	●		●			●
PRAWN	●	●		●	●	
SCAMPI	●	●		●	●	
SHRIMP	●	●		●	●	

Molluscs

	Boiling/Poaching	Steaming	Baking	Shallow frying	Deep frying	Grilling
COCKLE	●					
MUSSEL	●		●			●
OYSTER	●		●	●		
SCALLOP	●	●		●		●
SQUID	●			●	●	●
WHELK	●					
WINKLE	●					

INDEX